The Consequences of Love

The Consequences of Love

GAVANNDRA HODGE

MICHAEL JOSEPH

an imprint of

PENGUIN BOOKS

MICHAEL JOSEPH

UK | USA | Canada | Ireland | Australia
India | New Zealand | South Africa

Michael Joseph is part of the Penguin Random House group of companies
whose addresses can be found at global.penguinrandomhouse.com

Penguin
Random House
UK

First published 2020

002

Copyright © Gavanndra Hodge, 2020

The moral right of the author has been asserted

Picture credits: plate section page 1, top left, Alamy; centre left, Topfoto; page 7, top, Dan Burn-Forti

Set in 13.5/16 pt Garamond MT Std
Typeset by Jouve (UK), Milton Keynes
Printed and bound in Great Britain by Clays Ltd, Elcograf S.p.A.

A CIP catalogue record for this book is available from the British Library

ISBN: 978-0-241-41332-6

www.greenpenguin.co.uk

For Candy Hodge, 1979–1989

Infandum, regina, iubes renovare dolorem,
Troianas ut opes et lamentabile regnum
eruerint Danai, quaeque ipse miserrima vidi
et quorum pars magna fui.

Terrible, O queen, is the sadness that you
    ask me to recount,
of the Trojans, their wealth, their lamentable
    kingdom,
torn down by the Greeks, awful things which
    I myself saw,
and in which I played a large part.

                                    The Aeneid, Virgil

keep speaking the years from their hiding places.
keep coughing up smoke from all the deaths you
    have died.

                        'Therapy', Nayyirah Waheed

It seems to me, that if we love, we grieve. That's the deal. That's the pact. Grief and love are forever intertwined. Grief is the terrible reminder of the depths of our love and, like love, grief is non-negotiable. There is a vastness to grief that overwhelms our minuscule selves. We are tiny, trembling clusters of atoms subsumed within grief's awesome presence. It occupies the core of our being and extends through our fingers to the limits of the universe. Within that whirling gyre all manner of madnesses exist: ghosts and spirits and dream visitations, and everything else that we, in our anguish, will into existence. These are precious gifts that are as valid and real as we need them to be. They are the spirit guides that lead us out of the darkness.

Letter to a fan from Nick Cave,
on the death of his son

Prologue

1989, London and Tunisia

When you were nine you had a pink coat that you loved so much you wore it all the time, even on the early morning flight to Tunisia. It was long and thickly padded and made you look like a flamboyant Michelin Man, wedged into your window seat, the coat zipped right up under your chin. Mum bought it when it was too big for you and now it was too tight, but none of us could imagine a time when you would stop wearing it, however crazy it looked.

You didn't take your coat off until we were in the hotel room. You were sharing with Mum and Dad, sleeping on a camp bed in their room. You always shared with them. You didn't like to be alone.

You changed into your pink bikini, your tummy round and chubby, your chest still flat; Mum looked for your goggles and suntan lotion. You wanted to go for a swim immediately.

We found our holiday rhythm fast. Mum and Dad had their preferred sun loungers, and you would spend all day in the pool, white stripes of lotion on your cheeks. My friend Anya and I usually got up later so missed breakfast. I would order a pancake smeared with Nutella from the man who set up his stall at 11 a.m. every day – the aroma of the frying batter mingling with the seaweed smell of the sea. Sometimes you would see me queuing and join me, your bikini bottoms dripping with chlorinated water, thick wet curls stuck to your neck. 'Get me one too,' you would say, and you would stand there eating your pancake rolled like a cigar, the melting chocolate sliding down your fingers, handing me the greasy paper plate and running back to the pool, your wet footprints evaporating in the heat.

Sometimes we went to the local town. It had been smartened up for tourists and there were stalls selling brown leather shoes with curled toes and fluffy toy camels. We would walk along the middle of the dusty market road, you holding Mum's hand, Dad checking out every stall, me and Anya being propositioned by stall holders, offering five hundred camels, a thousand camels, a thousand camels and ten sheep.

'Five thousand camels and this one's yours!' Dad would shout, and I would punch him on the arm, furious.

'Ah, she has spirit,' the stall holders would say.

But mostly we sunbathed.

'This will set us up for the summer,' said Dad, comparing his mahogany-coloured forearm with my pale pink one, blotchy with sun rash.

In the late afternoons we would go back to our hotel rooms. You would have a nap, still in your damp costume and neon-green sunglasses. While you slept we would shower. I would wash off the suntan lotion, watch it spiral down the plughole, the steam billowing in clouds that filled the bathroom. Afterwards we would apply aftersun and get dressed.

Every night we ate dinner in the brightly lit hotel restaurant, crowded with shiny sunburnt people from all
over Northern Europe. You would pile your plate with
all sorts of mismatching things: sausages and pasta and
coleslaw and a great mountain of chips squirted with
ketchup. You would leave most of it, but you always finished your pudding; you even went back for seconds
of doughnuts, ice-cream and pink cakes with nuggets of
candied green fruit.

There were entertainments in the evenings: bingo,
shows, live music, a disco. One night Dad took you on
to the dance floor. The DJ was playing songs by the
Beatles. Dad held your hands and moved you left and
right, beaming at you as he lifted one of your arms above
your head, twirling you around, pulling you to him. You
laughed because you thought he would tickle you, but he
didn't, and you both kept dancing. Mum, Anya and I
were watching. Mum was clapping. It was the first time
you and Dad had danced together, they said afterwards.

When you came back to the table you were flushed
and excited.

'Dance with me,' you said, your brown eyes hopeful.

'No,' I said.

I was self-conscious and it was your bedtime. Soon
afterwards Mum took you up.

Later that night, past midnight, I was in bed reading,
the hotel quiet, my little lamp illuminating the pages of
my book. The sheets on the bed were cool and thick.
The maids tucked them under the mattress every morning so every night I had to kick them free.

There was a knock at the door. I didn't answer quickly enough so someone started turning the handle up and down loudly, as though they might break it.

'Gavanndra!'

It was Mum. She was shouting.

'GAVANNDRA!'

I got out of bed, walked to the door, my feet bare on the carpet. I opened the door.

Mum was in her blue cotton kaftan. Her face was pale, even though she had been sitting in the sun for a week. 'Candy's sick.'

I assumed it was a cold, a cough, a tummy bug, something like that. I couldn't understand why Mum had come for me. Maybe you'd asked for me, maybe you wanted us all to tend to you, our baby.

I walked the short distance to the room you shared with them.

I stood outside. I could hear coughing.

I held the door handle. I hesitated.

I opened the door. It was bright in there; all the lights were on. Dad was in his underpants, sitting on the double bed, his arms outstretched. You were running, one way and then the next, as though you were being hunted and you didn't know the way to safety. You were choking as you ran. A trickle of phlegmy blood dribbled down the side of your mouth, making a zigzagging trail of red spots on the carpet. Dad was trying to grab you, but you kept slipping from his fingers, as if you knew that if you stopped it would be over.

I was standing in the doorway. I didn't want to move,

4

but I felt Mum's hand on my back, pressing me into the room.

'I'm going to get help,' she whispered.

She went, shutting the door behind her. It was just the three of us.

Dad tried to catch you. 'Candy, my darling, you're gonna be all right. Candy. You've got to stop.'

Eventually he managed to grab you. You were slowing down, tiring, and he put his strong, brown arms around you and held you and you fell into him. He scooped you into his lap, cradling you like a baby, his legs wide apart. Your body was limp and floppy, your arms falling back over your head, your feet pointing downwards, and for a moment it looked like a sculpture, but Dad was howling, a noise tearing from his stomach, and I wanted to put my hands over my ears and close my eyes but I couldn't.

I couldn't move. I couldn't breathe. I couldn't stop watching.

Mum came back. There was more blood on the floor now, your body in Dad's arms, his contorted face, my frozen one, the scene so much worse than the one she'd left.

'There's a taxi,' she said.

Dad stood up, holding you, and walked, one solid footstep after another, bearing your weight.

'Hurry up,' said Mum.

In the back of the taxi Dad gave you the kiss of life, but this did not work. You were unconscious when you arrived at the hospital. A tracheotomy was performed but this made no difference. You did not regain consciousness.

You were killed by a rare airborne virus that shut down all your organs like lights going off in a house until everything went dark. After the autopsy they said that you could have caught the virus in London, it could have been working in your veins, hiding, multiplying, even as you got on the plane, wearing your pink coat.

They had to leave your body in the hospital. Mum and Dad said it was an awful place, you covered by a dirty blanket on a tiled floor. The staff tried to stop Mum kissing you goodbye, but she insisted.

The next morning Dad got out of bed, put on his holiday T-shirt and his holiday shorts. He walked down to the bar area of the hotel where the photographs that had been taken by the hotel photographer of the night before were routinely laid out. He found all the pictures of you, pictures of you clapping and dancing, and put these in his pocket. Then he took a bottle of Scotch whisky from behind the bar. He had not drunk proper alcohol for five years, not since giving up heroin, not since rehab, but the morning after you died he walked along the carpeted corridors swigging whisky. The alcohol slid down his throat and burnt his heart, making it sizzle. He opened the door to the room, your bikini still hanging from the hook in the bathroom, your sunglasses still on the dressing table. He sat at the end of the bed and finished the bottle. He burped once and then fell backwards. The bottle rolled from his fingers. Mum got out of bed, picked up the bottle, placed it on the side table.

Dad slept that whole day. Passed out.

Mum did not return to drink. Instead she went to the beach and she howled. Then she cried out to God. 'You'll have to help me because I can't deal with this!'

The day ended and a new one began as though nothing had changed. Normal things continued to happen, like sleeping and going to the loo and getting dressed, hunger and thirst. But we now understood that nothing was normal. We understood that the world is crazy because it is a world in which people exist one minute and do not the next.

Mum asked Anya to help fold and pack your clothes, because such things still needed to be done. I tried to help by floating in the swimming pool, wearing sunglasses, filling my plate at the dinner buffet with inappropriate things, squirting the lot with tomato ketchup, trying to show Mum and Dad that I could be both of us. I wanted to fill the gap left by you, even if it was just for this moment, so we could get through the impossible days.

It didn't work. They didn't even notice.

When the plane landed at Gatwick I wanted London to be grey, damp, cold. I didn't want to feel the sun on my skin any more. But when we touched down I saw the heat haze rising from the smooth black tarmac and I knew that it was not over, that nothing would make this feeling go away.

That night, when we turned on the television, the film *Don't Look Now* was showing. Donald Sutherland was staggering with the weight of his drowned daughter, who was wearing her favourite red raincoat. We turned off the television.

Your body came back to England a few days afterwards and was taken straight to a funeral parlour on the Fulham Road.

'Here she is,' said the man, opening the door to a room in which the lights had been dimmed.

A coffin was balanced on a plinth.

Mum and Dad were tense and formal walking into that room, their muscles ready for some fresh terror, but their bodies softened the moment they saw you, their little girl, funny, childish, loving, artistic, wilful, curious, sleeping deeply.

'There you are, my baby,' Dad said, and he cupped his hand gently to your cheek, which was not really a cheek any more, because it was cold and solid with embalming fluid. Mum gripped the edge of the coffin and said, 'Candy,' as though you were alive, as though you were lying there alive, looking beautiful.

I could not do that. I looked in, glimpsed your face, saw the strange softness that comes just before decay. I saw all the artifice, the make-up, the smile made by men in white laboratory coats pushing at the corners of your mouth, a child transfixed in a plastic moment, dead but not dead, hyper-real, rouge on your cheeks, pink lipstick on your lips, your eyes shut, your long brown eyelashes brushing your cheeks.

I found a chair in the corner of the room where I sat straight-backed, my eyes open but my sight turned inwards so that I did not see, my ears closed over so that I did not hear.

*

A week later we had your funeral. The windows were open so that the hotness of the city, the swirling dust that they said had come all the way from the Sahara, blew into my room along with the smell of rotting food.

I wore a long blue skirt and a blue jacket, new clothes that Mum had bought for me. I went into the hallway where they were waiting. The sight of them was so awful: Dad in his suit with a pink handkerchief in the top pocket, his hair newly washed and brushed back, his skin already sweaty at the temples; Mum all in black, black patent high heels, painted fingernails, but no mascara on her short, blonde eyelashes.

We walked down the steps, a family reconfigured, three instead of four. Outside there was a long black hearse which gleamed like a freshly groomed horse. You were in the back, in your own special place, with wide windows so everyone could see you, packed away in your little coffin. There were two wreaths, one in the shape of a teddy bear made out of pink roses, another of white roses, spelling out your name. *Candy.*

Two men in smart suits and black caps were waiting, ready to open the car door for us.

I had not realized that death was so grand.

I was very aware of you behind my head, that this was the last time you would be with us. After this we would never travel in a car together again, we would never do anything together again.

We arrived at St Mary The Boltons, which was like a village church, with its low stone wall and flower beds. We stood in a line and greeted the people who arrived, all the familiar faces, and it couldn't help but feel like an exciting social occasion, except that everyone I said hello to, everyone I hugged and patted on the back, everyone was crying, every face was blotched with tears, and some of them stayed in my arms and their shoulders shook, as if I could help them, me, sister of a dead girl. And I didn't cry, I don't know why, but the leaves fluttered in the trees, raining their golden droplets of sun, and the air was warm and my tears didn't come. I didn't even feel a tightness in my throat or a heaviness in my eyeballs. I thought that there must be something wrong with me that I felt nothing, and this was a terrible secret that I could not share.

Eventually everyone arrived and we walked into the church. Organ music was playing and sunlight was streaming through the stained-glass windows, making bright beams of yellow, blue and red. There were huge bunches of flowers tied with thick, trailing white ribbons at the end of each pew. The place was packed. I had been to weddings in this church before and never seen it so full.

We walked all the way to the front. Once we were seated they brought you in, carried on the shoulders of four men provided by the funeral company. You were placed on a little wooden stand so everyone could see. Mum was sitting between me and Dad. She reached for our hands and she gripped mine so tightly that her fingernails broke the skin of my palm.

The priest talked and then we sang 'All Things Bright and Beautiful', like at a school assembly. After that your school friends read a poem. I don't remember what the poem was; I don't remember any of the words that were spoken, only the looks on the people's faces, the flowers and the colours.

You left first, carried out of the church. We walked behind, our eyes lowered, watched by everyone. Our next destination was the crematorium, a magnolia-painted room with lots of empty chairs and the metal runners on which your coffin was carefully placed. Only a few people joined us there, family members, a couple of friends, one of the waiters from the Italian restaurant where we went for lunch every Saturday and some Sundays too, who had known you all your life.

We sat in our uncomfortable seats and listened as the machine whirred into life. We watched as your coffin moved towards the red curtains and passed through them into the furnace beyond. I was sure I could hear the roar of newly fed flames, even though the song '(I've Had) The Time of My Life' from the film *Dirty Dancing* was playing very loudly.

We got back into the hearse for the final drive home. There was nothing in the boot of the car now; the wreaths were burnt along with you.

The car pulled up outside our mansion block. It was lunchtime but I didn't feel hungry. The thing we had all been dreading, anticipating, planning, was done and now we were expected to get on with our lives.

One of the funeral company men opened the door for us and we got out, my father, my mother, me. The other man approached us. He was holding a rectangular wooden box – your ashes, I realized, and I wondered if they were still warm, like a freshly baked loaf of bread.

The man stood in front of Mum and held the box out for her to take. She looked at him, looked at the box, seemed confused at first, and then her face crumpled into pink wetness.

Dad stepped forwards. He took the box, tucked it under one arm and placed the other hand on the smart funeral man's shoulder. 'Thanks for everything you've done today, mate.' He handed over a pre-folded twenty-pound note.

'Come on, my darling,' he said as he walked towards the front door, you snug under his arm.

Mum and Dad bought a beautiful Chinese box made from golden lacquered wood inlaid with floral patterns. The box was waist height and had a big bronze key with a silky red tassel. They filled this box with all the things of yours that they could not bear to lose: your favourite soft toys and the hood of your pink coat.

They put the box containing your ashes on the mantelpiece in the living room and they kept the Chinese box in their bedroom.

We put you in wooden boxes, Candy. We locked you away.

I

2014, London

It is a chilly Tuesday in half-term. My daughters and I have been in the Horniman Museum admiring animals stuffed over one hundred years ago and fixed in dramatic poses. After an hour of chasing my children, shouting their names – 'Hebe! Minna! Come back here!' – I want to go home, but as we walk to the bus stop they spot the playground and insist on staying out a bit longer. I relent: better that they are outdoors than at home watching television. I buy a cup of tea from the lady in the corrugated hatch and settle on the low concrete ledge at the edge of the sandpit, watching my two girls. I watch them play and fight, fight and play, climb, swing, laugh, cry. They are three and six, so interwoven with each other, physically and emotionally. They share a bedroom; they loll on the sofa together, eat together, argue and tease, laugh and cuddle. And while I am sitting there, watching them, thinking of cheerfully mundane things like what I might cook for dinner, I have a realization that is like a shot of frozen air into my veins. My realization has different parts, a beginning, a middle and an end, but these parts hit me all at once, with no beginning, middle, end.

I realize that the age gap between my girls is almost the same as the age gap between me and my sister. I realize that what I am so enjoying watching, this connection between them, was something that I must have once had. I realize that I can't remember ever having that. In fact, I realize, I can't remember my sister, not at all. Apart from one moment: her death.

I sip my tea, trying to return the warmth to my body. I don't like the ice in my veins, the numbness in my fingers. Life is good. I have a job, a home, a family. I feel safe and loved. This desolating fear, this belongs to the past.

We get the bus home. I feed my children, bathe them, filling the bath with sparkly unicorns and plastic dinosaurs. I put them to bed, do their stories. Hebe can already read to herself; Minna prefers to pretend to eat the pictures of food in her favourite books, sweets and ice-cream and multi-tiered Moomin birthday cake. I sing to them, kiss them, tuck them in. Once the girls are settled I cook dinner. My husband Mike comes home from work. He edits the *New Review* magazine at the *Independent on Sunday* newspaper, the place where we first met, when I was a features editor and he was on the arts desk, an email-heavy office flirtation that segued via snogging in the back of a minicab on the way home from the Christmas party into marriage and children.

We eat roast chicken and share a bottle of red wine. I tell Mike about the museum and how the girls never seemed to be in the place where I last saw them, always running away, so curious and bold. We laugh about this and clean the dishes. We watch television, we go to bed, embrace before we fall asleep. And when I wake I still can't remember my sister. I can't remember my sister's voice, I can't remember a conversation with her, a moment we played together, even though I shared a bedroom with her until I was eleven. I have a photograph of her in which she wraps her arms around my waist and looks up at me. I am wearing headphones, my red Walkman hanging from the waistband of my shorts. I remember the feeling of those foam headphones against my ears, a squeaky sensation, almost like fingernails on a blackboard. But I can't remember how it felt to hug her, her arms tight around me, mine around her. And if I can't remember Candy, who will? We live on in the memories of those who love us, and I can't even perform this basic familial duty. I feel guilty because of this, on her behalf, but I also feel sad for myself. I had a sister, but I have lost her, twice, once when she died and again when I forgot her.

The really crazy part of all this is that I have an excellent memory. As a schoolgirl it was almost photographic. I could read an essay twice and then regurgitate it in an exam, one word leading to the next like fingers over piano keys. I can still remember the lyrics of nearly every song I listened to in my teens and twenties. It freaks out my husband when we drunkenly watch *Top of the Pops* reruns late at night and there I am, singing along to 'Marlene On The Wall', a song I haven't heard in three decades. I can remember what I ate for lunch with a friend years ago, even what we talked about. I can remember how my father's fingers felt against my neck when he did my hair on my wedding day, his belly pressed against my shoulder, his breath phlegmy and laboured, he was concentrating so hard. These are precise physical memories, traces of the past left on my skin, my father standing right by me, a man who died in 2009.

Yet there is this swirling, vertigo-inducing void where my sister should be. I can't believe I've never noticed it before, right there in front of me all this time. And now I have I cannot stop thinking about it.

We all responded differently to Candy's death. I remained numb, frozen by the shock of what I'd seen. This feeling did not fade; instead I adapted to it, like a sapling growing around a metal spike, making it part of who I was, not realizing this wasn't how a fourteen-year-old girl was meant to feel – detached and disconnected, unable to think about the sister I had lost without seeing a desperate, dying child.

My mother was not numb; she was raw. The love was still pouring from her and she needed somewhere to direct it. So she chose religion. That is what she saw when she stared out at the choppy North African sea. God. She found comfort in this new-found belief in the afterlife, a spangled heaven where Candy now was, and where Mum would find her again, one day, when the hell of this earth was left behind.

My father's approach could not have been more different. He chose a path that was seductive and familiar, one that he had been walking for many years. It was no surprise, really, that he was unwilling, unable even, to let himself feel the anguish of grief. He had never been able to endure emotional pain, and he knew the most perfect way to escape it.

2

1982, London

When I was seven years old I was shown a fire-safety film at my primary school in Chelsea. The teacher turned off the lights, pulled the curtains shut, and we all sat cross-legged in the dark on the floor, so close together our knees touched.

In the film it was nearly Christmas. There were presents under the tree, all wrapped with shiny ribbons and fat bows, presents of different sizes and shapes. The fairylights twinkled, on and off, on and off, even though everyone in the house was asleep and no one was there to see the lovely tree magically twinkling in the darkness. At the plug socket the wires were frayed, the plastic sheathing gone to reveal copper that sparked and hissed, tiny fireworks of blue and gold that leapt all the way to the presents, wrapped in crisp, flimsy paper that caught light. And so the fire began, a burning tree, the curtains catching and exploding, a silent blazing and smoke creeping under doors, up stairs, into the bedrooms where the children slept, a boy and a girl in neat single beds, the smoke curling into their nostrils and mouths, choking them while they dreamt.

The mother woke up and shook the father. They

covered their faces to leave the bedroom as the fire lapped up the stairs; they ran to the children's bedroom and shut the door behind them. The children were coughing, half awake, the fire outside the door. 'Don't touch the metal door handle!' shouted the father, and then, weirdly, in the film there was a scene in which one of the children did touch the door handle and they screamed as their skin melted and stuck to the hot metal. But this must have only happened in the imagination of the father, or one of the children, because then we watched the family crouching low, beneath the smoke, crawling on their unburnt hands and knees to the window. The father opened the window and they inhaled great lungfuls of cool, clean air. They shouted for help and the lights in the houses opposite came on so we knew that the fire engines would be on their way soon and no one would die.

When the firemen arrived they uncoiled huge, heavy hoses and sent up shiny ladders which the family climbed down, still in their night things. Their home blazed behind them, lighting up the night, but they were safe.

At the end of the film the chief fireman, his face sweaty and smudged with black, turned to the camera and addressed us, sitting there in our classroom. 'Make sure your fire alarm is working! Know your fire escapes!'

The teacher switched off the television and opened the curtains. I turned to look at my friends, eyes wide with shock. I hadn't realized I was in such peril. I lived in a flat on the third floor of a mansion block in Battersea. There were no fire escapes, so I couldn't know them. We didn't have a fire alarm, so I couldn't check if it worked.

After I saw that film I worried every night about what would happen if there was a fire in our flat. There were always things burning at home – candles and incense. There were always people in the sitting room smoking cigarettes. Our sitting room, with its broken light fittings hanging by tangled wires from the walls, the lamps with bits of coloured fabric thrown over them, the silk singed from the heat of the bulbs.

One night, not long after I saw the film about the house fire, I lay in bed reading an Enid Blyton adventure story I had borrowed from the school library, the pages soft from use, the spine cracked. I had a loose milk tooth and while I read I nudged at it with my tongue, pushing it a little further each time, easing it free. While I read and nudged I listened for my mother in the next-door room. I listened to her sighing and to the creaking of the bed frame. I waited for a few moments before I put the book down, got out of bed, left the room and peered in at my mother. There she was, lying on her side, the duvet making a mountain range of her hips and shoulders. She always went to bed early; all the wine made her tired and clumsy. I shut her door and mine, walked along the hallway, following the noise of the television. Dad was sitting on the sofa. Balanced on his belly were a packet of Silk Cut cigarettes and his grey plastic asthma inhaler.

'Hello, Daddy,' I said, sitting down next to him.

'Hello, you!' he said.

Dad was watching an American film on television. A policeman was hitting a muscly man on the back with a big black stick. Dad put the asthma inhaler to his lips and pressed it down twice. There were always loads of inhalers around the flat, in bowls and on shelves, used ones under furniture and new ones in drawers, funny little alien soldiers. I took the one from Dad's hand and pressed it, feeling the cold gas on my hand.

'I didn't have them when I was little. When I was little and I had a bad attack my mum – Grandma – she would lie on the carpet with me and wait for me to start breathing again.'

I put the inhaler back on his stomach. 'I've got another wobbly tooth,' I said.

'Ooh, let's see.'

I opened my mouth and pushed the tooth out as far as it would go, straining the thin strings of flesh that held it in place until they ached.

'Yucky!' he said, and before I knew what was happening he had grabbed a canister of squirty cream from the shelf next to him. 'Open your mouth!' He pushed the nozzle down and the cream sprayed out, making a gassy churning sound, expanding as it filled my mouth. I was laughing and choking at the same time, trying to swallow the cream as it oozed out of the edges of my mouth. Dad was squirting the cream into his own mouth now, overfilling it so there was a twirling peak, sucking it in. He put the cream back on the shelf. I could still feel the laughter in me and I could still taste the sweet cream. He lit a cigarette and my cat jumped on to the sofa, pressing her body against my leg, vibrating with purrs.

I loved being alone like this with Dad, late at night.

The doorbell rang. Dad sprang out of the sofa. He was bouncy and quick, not languid and slow like Mum.

'Come on up!' he shouted into the intercom.

He opened the door. I heard voices floating up the stairs.

On the glass-topped coffee table there were ashtrays, wine bottles, a record sleeve with a photograph of a blue mermaid on a rock, a wooden box with an Egyptian eye carved on the lid, and the scales. The scales were small, solid and nimble, with hinges and pins and tiny chains holding the plates. The weights were metal elephants of decreasing size that could be arranged in a line, like the scene in *The Jungle Book*. The elephants had been handled so much that the tops of the trunks were rubbed to a bright smooth bronze, while the feet and the legs were black with grime. 'They are from Thailand,' said Dad when he found me playing with them one day. 'They are really old, special, be careful with them.' Some of the weights were used more than others; some of the trunks were more shiny than others: the gramme, the 5 gramme. Those were the ones that got used the most.

Two men walked into the sitting room. They were skinny and tall, with tufty unbrushed hair that grew past their ears, pale skin and tired eyes with purple shadows beneath.

'So the Afghani stuff arrived,' Dad was saying. He was shorter and stockier than them, more energetic, more alive.

'Fabulous,' drawled Michael, hardly moving his mouth because he had the end of a cigarette hanging from between his lips. He sat down and reached forward to pour wine into a red KitKat mug that had once come with an Easter egg. His slender fingers were brown at the tips.

'Hi, darling,' he said, spotting me. I'd moved to a cushion in the corner of the room so that I could watch them. I folded my legs under me, so my long white nightie covered my toes.

'Hello,' I said.

'Well, get it out before everyone else gets here, first dibs and all that,' said Quentin, who was taller and thinner than Michael.

The doorbell rang again. Dad went to answer it.

'Hello there,' said Quentin, blowing me a kiss before he sank to his knees, pulling a black lump of something from his pocket. 'Daddy won't mind if I borrow some Rizla, will he?'

'No, that's fine,' I said.

A girl arrived next. She had lots of hair, which was blonde and silky and covered the faces of Michael and Quentin when she bent down to kiss them hello. I worried that perhaps her hair might go up in flames when she kissed Michael because the cigarette was still burning between his lips. Some of the tobacco that Quentin was sprinkling on the Rizla paper went on to the carpet when he lifted his face up to her. 'Hello, darling.'

They said this a lot. 'Hello, darling.' I don't think the word 'darling' meant that much to them. Dad said it differently. He said 'Hello, my darling' and the 'my' seemed important.

Her name was Sarah but Dad called her Lady Sarah and she always told him to stop being silly.

She slumped down on to the sofa next to him. She had diamonds in her ears that sparkled like Christmas.

Dad lit a cigarette and handed it to Sarah. She put it in her mouth and when she took it out the butt was glossy and red from her lipstick.

'Get Lady Sarah a proper glass for her wine, will you? She doesn't like drinking out of mugs.'

'Oh, Gavin,' said Sarah, slapping him gently on the thigh, but she looked at me and smiled, as if to say, Yes, I would prefer a proper glass.

I went to the kitchen. Dirty dishes were half submerged in greasy sink-water. A bottle of milk was open on the work surface and jaunty little silver fish were sliding along the grooves between the tiles. It smelt of week-old cat litter, even though the window was open.

I got on to a stool and found the cleanest-looking glass in the cupboard. I carried it into the sitting room as though it was a precious goblet. Sarah was standing by the record player.

'Ooh, I love this one,' she said, slipping a record out of its cover and laying it on the turntable. Dad turned down the volume on the television with the remote control, but he didn't turn it off, so the people were still there on the screen. The man was in the forest now, his face covered with mud; he was grabbing another man from behind and holding a knife to his throat, but we couldn't hear what they were saying to each other, we could hear music instead.

I filled the glass with red wine from the bottle that was now nearly empty and handed it to Sarah. I enjoyed performing these small tasks. I knew that if I was helpful and didn't get under their feet then I wouldn't get sent to bed.

Dad was kneeling by the table, reaching for the Egyptian-eye box.

They all stopped talking and watched, their breath stalled in their throats. He flipped open the lid. Inside was a plastic bag of light brown powder. There was also a smaller bag of white powder that was like icing sugar and a lump of black stuff the size of a plum.

'So, who wants what?' he asked.

'One for me,' said Sarah.

'One for me – no, two, and a gramme of the coke too, please. I've got a family thing in Wales tomorrow,' said Michael.

'Two for me as well, and another one for everyone,' said Quentin.

'Great,' said Dad.

We watched as Dad set to work, arranging the elephants, using his little plastic scoop to get just the right amount of powder on to the tiny bronze scale, tipping the powder into one of the small squares of paper that he had prepared, folding them up into fat rectangles and writing on the front with my green felt-tip pen: 'S1', 'M2', 'Q2'. As he was writing on the packets everyone was getting out their wallets and purses, pulling out notes, folding them over. It would be fun to have a cash register for this bit, I thought.

Dad collected the money, handed over the little packets, and then measured out a final gramme, Quentin's present to everyone.

I could sense their anticipation. It was like electricity. I felt it too. My heart was beating faster, even though I was sitting very still. But they were not still, they played with lighters, examined their hands, jiggled their feet. They tapped their cigarettes against the ashtrays, sometimes missing and spilling molten crumbs. I would watch as these crumbs burned out. Sometimes I would spring up and stub one out with my toe. The next day there would be another little black plastic crater in the carpet.

Dad tipped the powder on to the record cover. There was a roll of silver foil on the floor. It was so big and heavy, like a lump of actual metal, but thin sheaves of foil could be unrolled from it and torn off.

'Dig in,' Dad said.

They didn't jostle, they were polite, but I could tell they were impatient. They let Sarah go first; Dad tore the foil for her, a piece not quite as long as a book, and made a crease along the middle. She filled it with a big pinch of powder and took a lighter from the table. Dad had a rolled-up fifty-pound note for her and she creaked back into the seat in her tight jeans and held the lighter under the silver foil. Soon everyone was doing this, cooking their powder as the *Emotional Rescue* album played. No one spoke. The powder began to melt, transforming into an oozing golden liquid which bubbled at the edges. It was viscous like hot glass and started to blacken just before the smoke rose. It smelt like burnt sugar and swimming pools. They watched, their faces intent, holding the rolled-up notes, ready to catch the thick yellow fumes as they curled up. They dragged the smoke into their lungs, like a genie being sucked into a bottle. They did this until there was no more smoke, then their hands fell to their laps, hot scraps of foil in their limp fingers. They leant their heads against the sofa and each other while I watched, worrying at my tooth. Time folded in upon itself. The air was thick and spicy with cigarette smoke, heroin fumes, the incense from the sticks which were now burnt down, the candles overflowing with molten wax. They closed their eyes, deep in their own heads. I felt drowsy too, tired because I was small and had been at school all day and it was nearly midnight. Tired because everyone in the room was so sleepy and the atmosphere snuck in behind my eyeballs and made them glassy. When I got tired like this my knees would ache, a pain that was inside the bones. I knew that if I closed my eyes the pain would go away. It would be so lovely, so comfortable, with the muffled music and the soft cushions and my skin which I couldn't feel any more.

But I had to stay awake. I had to be vigilant. I couldn't relax like them. We didn't have a fire alarm or a fire escape.

The record finished, so that it was just turning and turning and making a click, click, click noise. I stood up, shaking off the spell, and turned it over. The music started again and the doorbell went.

'Get that for me, my darling,' Dad murmured.

I had to stand on my tiptoes to make myself tall enough to reach the intercom.

'Hello,' I said.

'Is that my girl?'

'Yes!' I said. 'Come up!' and I pressed the button hard to let him in.

Andy was my favourite. He smiled and the corners of his sad, merry eyes crinkled when he saw me. He bent down to give me a kiss, dry and light on my cheek.

'Come on through,' I said. 'Everyone's in the sitting room.'

Dad and Sarah were whispering to each other, not quite ready for the full volume of their voices. The others were still zoned out.

I went back to my corner. Andy found a cushion and lowered himself down near me.

'How are you?' he asked.

'I'm OK. A bit tired. I've got sleepy knee again.'

'Poor thing,' he said. 'Shall I massage it better?'

'Yes, please.'

I stretched out my legs, my knees scuffed with old scabs, my feet striped with dirt from wearing plastic jelly-bean sandals all day. Andy closed his hands around my right knee first, rubbing it with his thumbs, firm and gentle; and then he moved on to my left knee. He stared down at my legs as he worked, concentrating.

'Is that better?' he asked.

'Yes, thank you,' I said.

They were waking up now, their fingers twitching.

'Hello, mate,' said Dad, as if he had only just noticed Andy was in the room. 'What can I do you for?'

'Three, please, and one for everyone.'

'Brill,' said Dad, because what was left from the last lot would not be enough for them all to have another go, even though Michael was still passed out, so there were only four of them. Dad often chucked a bit extra in the middle but he couldn't do this too much, he told me, because then he wouldn't make any money at all and he wouldn't be able to buy us new things like the roller skates we'd got the other week.

Dad measured out Andy's heroin and handed him the little packet with 'A3' written on it. Andy handed him the money across the table. He tore a strip of silver foil and sprinkled it with powder, shaking the foil a little so it made a thin line. This was the signal for them to have another turn, the same routine, the burning with the lighter, the powder turning to bubbling liquid, the yellow smell that was always in my nostrils, even when I wasn't in this room.

Their eyes fluttered shut; their heads lolled. Andy was laid out straight on the floor, his head on the carpet. He was breathing so softly, hardly at all.

'Helloooo. Is there anyone home?'

I started up from my position, crouching by Andy, my ear to his face, making sure he was alive.

It was John. Andy must have left the door open, so he had walked straight in without knocking or buzzing. He was just as thin as the others but he looked meaner, with his thin lips and hooded eyes.

'Some fucking party this is,' he said, and shoved Sarah's inert body along the sofa so he could sit down.

'They've just had some,' I said.

'I see. Do you know if Gav's got any coke? I'm trying to be a good boy,' he said, his restless gaze casting around the room as though cocaine might be hanging from the walls, or on display on the mantelpiece.

'I . . . I don't know. There is just what there is there,' I said, pointing to the plastic bags in the Egyptian-eye box.

John snatched the smaller bag from the box, twisted it open and stuck his pinky finger in, coating it with white powder. He put his finger in his mouth and sucked.

'That'll do,' he said and tipped the powder on to the glass table, using a loose razor blade to neaten it into a line. He got on to his hands and knees to snort the cocaine, not using a rolled-up note or anything. I watched, trying to work out how much he had taken. One elephant's worth? I wanted to be able to tell Dad, so he could get the right money.

'Aghhh!' He made a noise that was relief, pleasure and anger all combined, and then he looked at me. He didn't get back up on to the sofa. Instead he started to move around the table, walking on his knees, shuffling along the carpet.

'Has anyone ever given you a Chinese burn, a proper one?' he asked.

'No,' I said.

'Oh!' he said, and he kept moving towards me. He smiled and I saw that his teeth were mouldy brown. 'There's a real art to giving a proper one. It hurts like hell, really feels like burning, but it doesn't leave any sort of mark.'

I crossed my arms, tried to make myself as small and unassailable as possible. I looked at my father, his eyes closed, his mouth hanging open. I thought about school and the fun stories I told every Monday for Show and Tell. Stories about the nightclubs I went to, the models I met, the rock stars I danced with. Stories about champagne and cigarettes. 'What an incredible imagination your daughter has!' the teachers would say to my mother. 'Where is she getting all this from?' In the car home Mum would say, 'You must never tell them what really happens.' And she would hold my wrist so tight.

I wondered what I could say at school about tonight. Would I tell them that my dad had made friends with an aristocrat, and that he had invited us to his palace in the countryside, shown us secret rooms that normal people never got to see, with jewels and swords. Yes, maybe that was the story I would tell.

'Good evening, Jonathan,' said Michael, who was still lying on the carpet with his eyes closed, but, it seemed, had woken up.

John laughed. 'I've been looking for you!'

'Well, you know where to find me,' he said. He sat up and leant back against the sofa. 'You should really try this Afghani gear, it's incredible.'

'Oh fuck it, go on then.'

I didn't understand any of it, why they came to our house to take something that sent them to sleep, why they spent so many nights on our living-room floor, why they didn't just go to bed in their own homes, which were nicer than ours – I knew that, I'd seen them. I often went with Dad to drop packages off on a Saturday morning or a Sunday afternoon, driving over the river to their high-ceilinged flats in Chelsea and Mayfair. It didn't make any sense to me, and when I asked Dad he couldn't explain it either.

I was the only one awake now.

The film was finished. The television crackled with grey speckles.

The record was finished.

They were finished for tonight, I decided.

This was what I had been waiting for. I took the still-burning cigarette from between Andy's fingertips and stubbed it out in the ashtray. I stepped between their bodies, light on my toes, and I blew out the candles, pinched the wicks with my thumb and forefinger to be sure, checked that the incense sticks were cold, took the needle off the record. I turned off the TV and the screen turned black with an electric hiss. I opened the window just a little. The fumes rushed out into the night like escaping ghosts.

I looked at them all. They did not look comfortable, their skinny limbs all at strange angles, their heads too heavy for their necks. Apart from Dad – he always looked comfortable, nose to the ceiling, mouth open, snoring, stomach rising and falling, cash in his pocket, asthma inhaler in his fist.

My bedroom smelt of toys and milky breath.

I got into bed, sat there for a moment, pushing at my tooth. It was coming. I could feel it. There was a sharp needle of pain and then plop it fell into my open palm, a shiny baby tooth and one drop of blood. I slid it deep under my pillow, wiping my bloody hand on my sheet and closing my eyes. I soothed the ragged gum with my tongue, wondering how the fairy would manage to burrow her way under there. She would have to be very small and very strong.

It was a blink sleep, close your eyes and it is morning.

The tooth was still under my pillow. I was disappointed. I must have left it too late for the fairy.

Andy and Michael were asleep on the sitting-room floor, stretched out.

The Egyptian-eye box was gone.

The scales had been packed away and were back on the shelf.

The used bits of silver foil had been rolled into sticky balls and chucked into the cupboard behind the sofa.

The sun was shining and I was going to school where I had friends and the teachers liked me.

And I was happy because everyone was alive, everyone had survived the dark night, my sister and my mum, my dad and Andy; they had all slept safely.

I had made sure of it. Me. I was small and very strong.

3

2014, London

When I was a baby my father used to blow the smoke from his joint into my face to stop me crying and put a tot of whisky in my bottle to help me sleep.

That was a long time ago. I am not that person any more. In our ground-floor flat in South London there are two fire alarms, one in the kitchen and one in the hall, both wired to mains electricity so they don't need to be checked. My children are fed, showered, stories read and in bed by eight p.m. At night our house is dark and calm. In the morning the sitting room and kitchen are clean, ready for another bright, sunny day.

Breakfast is busy, toast and cereal, eggs fried, scrambled or dippy, getting the girls dressed, pulling up their grey woollen tights (lifting them off the ground by the waistband, swirling them round, 'flying tights!'), brushing their blonde hair into ponytails, somehow getting myself ready for work among everything. Make-up on, make sure there is no egg yolk on my top (just scrub it off if there is), leave the house at eight twenty on the dot, walk to the station (I hate being late, it makes me panic).

In the office where I work the walls are painted white and the desks are clean and white too. I am neat and together, in control, on top of everything. I am the deputy editor of *Tatler*, the oldest magazine in the world. A grand and solid institution (if perhaps a little frivolous). A grand and solid job (and a nice way to pay the mortgage). I've had it for a year. I wish Dad were alive to see it. He would have been proud; he would have lied and told everyone I was editor.

I like to get home by seven fifteen so I can put the children to bed. But sometimes when an article goes awry or deadlines loom, I have to stay late.

This is one of those nights. I am researching a story about the eighties Sloanes, a tribe lavishly depicted in the pages of *Tatler*. My research involves looking through old copies of the magazine. I have a great pile of them on my desk, bound in red leather with gold writing on the spines so that they look like dictionaries or encyclo-paedias, tomes containing important knowledge.

I am alone. The movement-sensitive lights in the ceiling wink off one by one until only the bulb above my head still shines.

I turn the pages, observing the strapless gowns, the ziggurats of champagne glasses, the heirloom tiaras, the uproarious and non-stop fun. *Tatler* is a magazine about aristocrats, royals, the rich, their houses, their pets. I am the daughter of a hairdresser from Bromley and a model from Woodford Green. My grandfather was an off-stone sub at the *News of the World*; my uncle was a butcher who once got into trouble for selling stolen meat; one aunt was a florist, another a waitress.

These are not my people.

But then I begin to see them. The ones who sat in my living room at night; the ones who bought heroin from my father and took it while I watched. They are all here: John, Quentin, Michael, Sarah, youthful and golden, not emaciated and nicotine-stained, not how I remember them. There are others I remember too, Jamie, Marquess of Blandford and Lady Alethea Savile. I find a portrait of her dressed in a silk ballgown, blonde hair blow-dried, lips shiny with pale gloss, seated in a beautiful blue and green tiled room. Dad cried when he discovered that she had died of a suspected drug overdose in her flat in Chelsea. Her twin brother Jonny, also a friend of Dad's, found her body after she died.

I was making my own breakfast by the time I was three, climbing on to the kitchen work-top to pull down packets of cereal, going into the living room to eat fistfuls of Rice Krispies out of the box in front of the television, the screen too close to my nose, the room dark, wine bottles and ashtrays all around, my parents still asleep – who knew when they would wake up.

My mother once told me that she and Dad were surprised to find themselves pregnant a second time because they had been so wasted on booze and drugs that they couldn't remember having had sex. I would have been nearly four years old when they conceived my sister. If they couldn't remember having sex, who was looking after me? (I don't ask this question; I don't want to upset her.)

They'd met late one night on the Embankment. Mum had been to a ball. She was a model, so she was probably paid to go, paid to look gorgeous. Sometimes she was paid to pretend to be the girlfriend of a person she barely knew, a European actor or film director who needed a woman on his arm for an event.

But on this night she'd had enough of pretending. She was standing on the street, waiting for a cab that never arrived, her toes numb in her high heels, her lacquered curls wilting. And along came Dad, driving his psychedelic Campervan, the Rolling Stones blaring from the stereo, his long hair dyed orange by henna and the Spanish sun. He was just back from three years in Marbella and the first person he saw in London was Mum, a gorgeous blonde in distress. He pulled over, the cars around him beeping in protest, and wound down the window. 'Hop in, love. I'll take you where you want to go.'

I was conceived not long afterwards. It was a hot King's Road afternoon, perfect for love-making by an open window, a round of applause at the end from the art-school students who had gathered to watch in the halls of residence opposite. The doctors told my parents they were having a boy. They were going to call me Gavin Junior. But when I was born a girl my dad made up Gavanndra, insisting on the two 'n's, even though the man at the register office told him he was spelling the name wrong. My mum chose my middle name, Layla, after her favourite song by Derek and the Dominoes.

My parents married two months after I was born. It was Mum's birthday. Dad had forgotten to buy her a present so asked her to marry him instead.

This is how my family began, chance and brazen

caprice, instability that has to become solid at some point, doesn't it, because otherwise there is nothing to build on, nothing that a child can be certain of.

I was that child.

My memories of my father's dealer days are not narrative, they are sensory: the toothache sweetness of the Alpen and Butterscotch Angel Delight mixture that was the only food he, a junkie, could eat; the dusty smell of the incense; the rough scratch of the kilim cushion material. I must have been a little high myself, dopy with heroin smoke, my hazy memories not so different to the fragmentary recollections of the other people there, the ones who lost a whole decade, often a whole life, to drugs. But I know it happened. I know I sat in the living room with those people night after night, watching them chase the dragon, snort coke, smoke joints, cleaning up after them, managing their chaos in my small, determined way. The story starts to knit together as I get a bit older, when I better understood what my father and his friends did every night. It was not what other people's parents did, I discovered once I started staying the night with friends and would creep around dark houses in which everyone was asleep by 11 p.m. (I would get scared, wake up the parents, tell them I wanted to go home). It was dangerous too, I discovered, the day a rival dealer tried to break into our flat, banging his fists against the door, kicking at it until the wood splintered. Dad pushed himself against the door, shouting: 'Fuck off! Fuck off!' Eventually the man gave up and left. Emotional intensity helps to set memory and fear is the most intense emotion of all because we have the most to learn from it.

I remember one night when I had grown larger, was less nimble, less able to fold myself quietly into a corner. They were all there, in our living room, more of them than usual, faces I didn't recognize. The coffee table was piled with various powders, the ashtrays full, the novelty mugs brimming with cheap red wine. I got up to move from one part of the room to another; I don't know whom or what I was going towards or getting away from, but I was ungainly in my fast-changing body and the space around the coffee table was a narrow obstacle course of cushions, glasses and outstretched limbs. I tripped, stumbled, reached out. My hand found the table and I leant on it to stop myself falling over. But like so much else in our flat the table was broken, the base not properly attached to the table-top, even though Dad had patched it with gaffer tape. The thick glass tipped beneath my weight, and all the heroin and cocaine, the wine, the ashtrays, everything on it began to tumble and merge, slipping off the table at once, fast and slow. They were shouting at me 'What the fuck are you doing?' as the thing they loved the most was lost in our stained old carpet, mixed with wine and warm ash and razor blades. They got on to their hands and knees and tried to salvage their beautiful heroin, but it was ruined and it was my fault and they all hated me. Even Dad.

That was a long time ago. I am not that person any more.

Sometimes, when my daughters can't sleep, they lie

in their bunk-beds and say to me, 'Mummy, I've got sleepy knee,' and I will take their aching legs in my hands and gently rub their small bones with my thumbs. And it is strange, this thread connecting the past to the present: my body, my memories, manifesting themselves in my babies. They must have got it from me somehow, this term, this feeling. Perhaps I once mentioned to them how long ago my legs used to ache in the night when I was tired and how I came up with my own special name for the feeling. I would not have explained the context.

It is strange because I have worked so hard to separate my past from my present. I have erected a wall between then and now, brick by brick, so that I may exist, be a wife, a daughter, a parent, a friend; so that I may sleep at night and wake in the morning looking forward to the day; so that my children will never know what I knew. When they go to bed they do not worry about flames engulfing their home or people dying from a drug overdose on the living-room floor. They are not afraid.

Because I have built this wall so purposefully and so well, when people meet me they do not see the daughter of a philandering junkie, they do not see the girl who watched her sister die in a hotel room in Tunisia, they see an articulate, educated, confident woman. They see success, not skin-of-the-teeth survival.

This is what I want them to see.

This is what I want to believe.

But now here I am, looking at pictures of the privileged

junkies who populated my childhood and unsafe memories are bobbing up from somewhere within me.

I thought I had found a place to hide from my past: this home, this family, this job, this life. What if I was wrong?

4

1984, London

Dad always thought he could get away with it, all the risks and chances, all the shortcuts and the lies. When the police came it was worse for us than him. He wasn't even home.

I was in my second year of junior school, the last lesson of the day, when Mr Mitchell walked back into the classroom, strolling with his hands in his pockets, his eyes roving until he spotted me. He wore red waistcoats and red-framed glasses and was my form teacher. I liked him, especially when he got so angry that his cheeks blazed as red as his waistcoat and he threw something, most often just a book or a pencil case, but once an actual chair. That made me laugh inside.

'Can I borrow you?' he said.

I thought perhaps it was a task he needed help with, although I couldn't imagine what – I wasn't good at much, not art, not sports. I was good at reading, but that was about it. I was reading *Lord of the Rings* for the third time. I loved the edition we had at home, the parchment-thin paper, the maps and strange alphabets. The way it was so straightforward who was good and who was bad.

I stood up. Mr Mitchell held the door open for me so

I had to pass under his arm to leave class. He let the door swing shut.

'There's been a problem at home.'

I opened my mouth.

'Nothing terrible,' he added. 'Not really. Just . . .' He paused. 'Just a situation. So I'm driving you back. Your mum will be there.'

His car was, of course, red. It was a VW Beetle, like ours, but shiny and tidy, no rubbish in the footwell, no tears in the fabric of the seats, no rusty bits or the key getting stuck in the lock.

I got in and was amazed at the springy perfection of the seats. 'Is your car new?' I said.

'No, I've had it seven years,' said Mr Mitchell.

But I could tell that he was pleased I'd asked.

It was a ten-minute drive home, quicker than usual because we missed the traffic.

'Goodbye, good luck,' he said.

I got out of the car and he watched me through the closed window, his seatbelt still on, the engine still running, as if he knew he was meant to make sure I got in the house OK, but wanted to get away as fast as he could.

I put my key in the lock, but before I pushed open the door, I turned around. Mr Mitchell was still there, waiting, watching. I waved. 'Goodbye!'

He looked sad, his red cheeks pale.

I walked up the stairs slowly. The block was quiet and my legs were heavy. When I finally reached the third floor I was surprised to find the door open.

Mum was standing just inside. 'You're here,' she said. She was pressing her fingers into her forehead as though she was in pain and her cheeks were blotchy from crying. 'They're in your bedroom. They won't listen to me.'

The flat was a mess. The flat was always a mess, but this was a different sort of mess: sofa cushions were tossed on the floor; bits of fabric had been pulled off the lamps; all the ornaments were tipped over. Nothing was in the right place, nothing was the right way up, everything was wrong.

I left my school bag on the floor by the door and went to my bedroom. I could hear two men talking.

'What's this?'

'Have you looked in here?'

I pushed the door open and saw that the voices belonged to two policemen in dark navy uniforms made of thick wool with shiny buttons. I saw that all my books had been thrown across the floor, the duvets had been pulled off the beds, clothes had been tossed from drawers. One of the policemen was by Candy's pile of soft toys. He had a pink Care Bear in one hand and a fistful of white stuffing in the other. He must have ripped it open, stuck his fingers into its belly, pulled it apart. He threw the bear and its insides on the floor, picked up another and pulled that one apart too. The plushy fabric made a ripping sound as it tore.

I knew what they were looking for and I knew it wasn't hidden inside one of my sister's teddies.

A couple of nights after a rival dealer had tried to break into the flat, banging on the door and swearing,

Dad and I had sat up together late into the night. We had no visitors; it was just us. Dad got his DIY bag out of the utility cupboard behind the sofa. It was a black sports holdall filled with rusty nails and old drills, a massive hammer and paintbrushes that were solid with dried emulsion.

'We've got to get a bit clever, you and me,' Dad said, puffing on a joint. 'There are all sorts of dodgy characters about.'

We hadn't discussed the man or what he might have done had he managed to get into the flat – steal the drugs, rob us, beat us up, kill us – but I knew that was what we were talking about.

Dad had the Egyptian-eye box open on the glass coffee table, three plastic baggies of powder squashed into it like nestling chicks. He plucked them out one by one and laid them on the table, then he plunged his hand into the DIY bag, something I was always too scared to do because of all the sharp metal and the malfunctioning power tools. He rummaged around a bit, Mary Poppins style, and brought out a big plastic torch with an orange casing and a black head. He unscrewed the head and let the three jumbo Duracell batteries slide into his hand. He chucked them into the DIY bag and then stuffed the three bags of heroin into the body of the torch, one by one, before screwing it shut. He turned the torch on and off and laughed when it didn't work.

'Don't tell anyone about this, G, it's our little secret.'

'Yes, Daddy,' I said, swelling with pride.

The other policeman, not the teddy-destroyer, stepped

up on to my bed, on top of the sheets, in his shiny black outside shoes with their thick soles, so that he could look behind the mirror.

'Excuse me,' I said. I was angry and that made me brave.

The policeman standing on my bed turned around. 'Please go back into the hall,' he said.

'What are you doing?' I asked.

'We are searching this property,' said the other policeman.

But I was still looking at the one who was on my bed. 'Don't you think you should take your shoes off before standing on someone's bed?' I said.

A funny look passed across his face and suddenly he didn't look so sure of himself. The other policeman looked at the white fluff that he had torn out of the belly of a teddy bear and I hoped that he felt bad too.

'Please go back into the hall.'

I shuffled back a little, but still I watched them.

The policeman stepped off my bed. 'It's not in here,' he said.

The other policeman let the ruined teddy drop to the floor.

I followed the policemen into the living room. It felt like a game of hot and cold, and they were getting warmer, warmer, warmer, but I kept my gaze calm and clear as they pushed the sofa into the middle of the living room and pressed the utility cupboard door so it swung open. Inside was the ironing board, a rarely used mop, an old stereo. The DIY bag was on one of the shelves, but the policeman got down on to his knees and started scrabbling around in the darkness. He found a rolled-up ball of silver foil and untwisted it to reveal its blackened, sticky heroin core.

'Put this with the rest,' he said.

Then he stood up and closed the utility cupboard door.

Colder, colder, colder . . .

That night I told Dad the story of the police raid, embellishing it and making it more exciting, emphasizing my bravery, my coolness under pressure, my poker-faced poise. He squeezed me hard. 'I'm so proud of you, my darling! We got away with it!' We ate crème caramel out of plastic pots to celebrate and Dad got the heroin from the torch, looked at it, chuckled and did a little bit, as a treat, even though he had got this lot in to sell and had promised Mum he would try to stop using, really try this time.

I ended up watching the telly by myself as he slipped away into unconsciousness, repacking the heroin into the torch, dropping it into the DIY bag, zipping it shut.

5

2014, London

I have been given the task of filling a new slot in the magazine called 'Women and Charity'. I must find four upper-class women who are prominent in the charity sector and talk to them about their work. Kate, *Tatler*'s editor, suggests Julia Samuel as the first subject. Julia is a psychotherapist and a founder patron of the charity Child Bereavement UK as well as a member of the Guinness family. She was the first resident psychotherapist at Paddington Hospital, caring for parents grieving the loss of babies in childbirth. She was also great friends with Princess Diana and, apparently, consoled the young princes William and Harry after their mother's awful death.

We meet at Julia's Bayswater flat, which is at the top of many flights of carpeted stairs. Julia has short blonde hair and blue eyes. She is brisk but not unfriendly, offering me a cup of tea and inviting me to sit at her kitchen table. I get out my Dictaphone and notepad full of careful research. I am very professional and serious with my spectacles and my smart blue dress from Whistles.

Julia does not want to talk about Princess Diana, she wants to talk about the charity. She explains how CBUK supports children who have been affected by the sudden death of a loved one and tells me about the work the charity does in schools, giving teachers the tools to communicate with bereaved children via workshops and informative literature. I pretend to concentrate; I nod and ask pertinent questions, even though my eyes are too wide and my heartbeat too fast. Julia occasionally goes silent, watching me. I feel a little uncomfortable when she does this.

'Did something happen to you, Gavanndra?' she asks.

I open my mouth to say: 'No! What are you talking about? Let's keep talking. What was Princess Diana really like?'

But those are not the words that come out.

I tell her about Candy. My voice cracks but I do not cry.

Julia listens; then she says how sorry she is for the things I have seen and experienced, how sorry she is for my whole family. 'But you have all this suppressed grief, you really should see someone.'

'Yes,' I say. 'I will.'

I do not tell Julia the worst of it. I do not say that I cannot remember Candy.

I do remember, just before Candy was born, walking around the flat with my mother, her huge belly straining against the fabric of her nightie, and telling her that we needed to make the house safe for my new sister, pointing at dangerously sharp ornaments, the ashtray that had to be moved to a higher shelf so she wouldn't eat the cigarette butts, things that could cut her, burn her, hurt her.

'Oh yes, we must move that, you're right. Good girl.'

I remember going with my mother to the World's End Nursery to pick up a kitten, a companion for me so that I would not feel left out when my new sister arrived. I chose a tiny tabby with three freckles on her wet nose. I called her Spottynose and we carried her home in the plastic shopping bag which also contained cat food and cat litter, her little face poking out of the top.

I can remember all this, but I cannot remember a baby, a cot in my room, a small strong fist.

Even once Candy was born I am alone in my memories, never with my sister.

I remember one holiday in Puerto Banús. We were staying in a small holiday complex, a rectangle of villas surrounding a pool. Candy would have been just over a year old, but I was playing by the pool by myself, no parents, no adults. I was jumping in and out of the pool, loving the splashing, the cool water, the feeling of sinking, pulling myself out and plunging back in again, running at the pool, curling myself into a ball, divebombing and belly-flopping. I was a confident swimmer, a happy holidaymaker who knew a few words of Spanish and enjoyed plates of clams followed by a chunk of water-melon bigger than my face. I was such a confident swimmer that my parents were content to leave me by a pool, alone, aged five, running along the slippery tiled edge, floating at the bottom, eyes open, to see how long I could hold my breath.

I was a confident swimmer. What could go wrong? I jumped in the pool backwards. I misjudged the distance and my chin cracked against the concrete edge, knocking me unconscious, splitting my chin open, skin flapping away from jawbone. I sank to the bottom and the water turned red with my blood as no one watched.

I am alive because of chance. A young man happened to open the door of his villa, saw the strange redness that was spreading in the pool – my blood, becoming thin and diluted with chlorinated water. He leapt into the pool and pulled me out, dragged me on to the side, pumped my chest so that water spurted and spluttered from my mouth, the sun bright overhead.

I was not aware of any of this happening. This is what I have been told. The next thing I knew I was in hospital, Dad staring down at me, grinning, the long gold chain that he always wore dangling above my nose.

'Hold still, my darling, let the man sew you up.'

I would never leave my girls alone by a pool. I don't like to let them out of my sight. I hover close to them in the playground, shout at them when they run too far ahead. I tell them not to cycle too fast, climb too high, go too far out in the sea. At night I check there is nothing too tight around their necks. I listen to their breathing in the dark and lay my hand on their chests to make sure they are still warm. I imagine all the ways they could die. I am afraid. The fear lives in me, but I keep it hidden. No one knows the strange thoughts that eddy in my head, not my husband, not my best friends; I keep these thoughts to myself because they are horrible and ugly and I don't think other people should have to hear them. It might make them think I am horrible and ugly too.

I do not arrange to see someone to talk about Candy, even though I told Julia Samuel I would.

6

1984, London and the South Coast

'Write him a letter,' Mum said after another police raid. 'Ask him to stop taking drugs. Ask him to do it for you.'

I found a nice sheet of paper, thick and unlined. I wrote him a letter. I put my all into it, heart and soul, right there on the page. I told him how much I loved him, I told him that I didn't want him to die or go to prison. I told him we needed him and that was why he had to stop taking drugs. Please, Daddy.

I ended the letter with the signature that I had been practising.

I folded the letter many times, knowing that the more something is folded the more powerful it is. I left the letter on his pillow. I didn't see him read it, but the next day we went for a walk in the park, just the two of us. He wore a long coat and kicked at the grass even though the leaves had not yet fallen. His voice was thick when he finally spoke, the hard words sticking in his throat.

'I'm going to do it, I'm going to stop taking drugs,' he said.

'Good,' I said, and I didn't cry because we were talking like grown-ups.

'Not all drugs, obviously, just heroin, just my drug of choice, I'm never going to take that again,' he said.

'Of course, I understand.'

I didn't really understand. But I did understand that my words had made something important happen.

Dad had to go away to stop taking drugs. After a month we went to visit him. Mum didn't say much during the train journey; she just stared out of the window as the grey changed to green.

When we arrived I discovered that the sea in England is not glittery blue like on holiday. The sea in England is the colour of hot chocolate and the sky is low with heavy clouds.

'Go and tell that taxi driver where we are going,' said Mum.

I was so excited to see Dad again.

The driver had the radio on, music playing loud, and Mum said, 'Can you turn that down?'

I saw the driver looking at Mum in the rear-view mirror.

I knew what he saw. I saw it too. In the weeks since Mum had stopped drinking wine she had seemed sad and lifeless. Her hair was often greasy and there were spots of food on her baggy jumper. When she did wear make-up the mascara would soon slide off her eyelashes and stick to the skin under her eyes like broken spiders' legs. I couldn't understand where my funny, giggly Mum had gone, the one who, when we were in the park, would tell me that she wasn't wearing any knickers under her wafty purple skirt because it made her feel free and daring.

Mum made the driver take us all the way up the bumpy, crunchy gravel driveway to the entrance of the building. It looked like a boarding school, big and gloomy. I undid my seatbelt and got out of the car while she was paying. I wanted to run up the stairs, open the front door. I wanted to find him.

'Hang on,' Mum said.

There were two people sitting on a bench outside the building: one held his head in his hands between his knees; the other was smoking a cigarette, tapping constantly even when there was no fresh ash to fall.

We walked up the steps together. I pushed the door open – no need to knock or turn a handle. It had been painted white, but the paint was old and cracked. If I'd had a bit of time I could have peeled it all off.

Dad!

He was standing just inside, in the hallway, his hands in his pockets, looking at his feet.

'Gavin,' said Mum.

He looked up. 'Hello, gang,' he said. He smiled, but it was not one of his proper smiles. His skin was flabby on his face and it looked as though his clothes didn't belong to him. I wanted to hug him, to make him right.

'Hi, Dad!' I said.

'My girls,' he said, and he pulled me in for a cuddle, squashing my face into his belly. He reached out for Mum and pulled her in too. This was what we called a group hug, but Dad smelt funny, as if he had been using different soap or something, so I didn't close my eyes.

'Come and see everyone,' he said.

We followed him through a door into a large room with sofas and chairs. Tall windows looked out on to the gardens and there was a big blackboard with people's names written in white chalk. Gavin, Michael, Catherine, Quentin. Next to the names were comments like 'Needs to work on his temper', 'It's OK to cry' and 'Talk to us'. Thin people in baggy clothes were gripping mugs of tea, reading books or writing on bits of paper. There was a table with a kettle and a couple of biscuit tins.

'Biscuits!' I said, and I chose two chocolate bourbons, putting one into my pocket for later.

In an armchair close to the table I saw Lady Sarah. She was wearing no make-up and had lots of spots. 'Hi!' I said, my mouth full of biscuit.

She held my cheeks with her dry fingertips. Her breath smelt horrible. 'Hello, darling, bit of a change of scene, isn't it?'

I was pleased when we left that room. We walked along corridors and up staircases.

'Jamie was here last week,' said Dad. 'Was doing all right. But then he ran away, couldn't take it any more, climbed over the bloody wall, can you believe it? Have you seen the size of it? Amazing!'

There were lots of doors. Some were closed, some open; inside I saw beds and desks, people sitting at desks and people lying on beds. From behind the closed doors I could hear groans. My stomach felt strange and

I decided to save my second biscuit for the train journey home.

'This is me!' said Dad, stopping outside a door.

His room was small and rectangular. There was only one window, a narrow bed with a scratchy-looking brown blanket, a cupboard, a chest of drawers, a chair and desk with pens and pieces of paper covered with big, round handwriting. Mum went to the window and stared out of it, her back to us.

'So, yeah, this is where it all happened, these four walls, sweating and shitting for days, worst cold turkey ever. There was one bit where I really believed that I had tiny insects living under my skin, ants, or caterpillars, something with loads of legs anyway. Hallucinating, the shakes, the lot. They just give you a plastic bucket and tell you to get on with it. Do it the hard way, so you won't want to do it again, which is bullshit, of course.'

He smiled at me. I was thinking of caterpillars and all their legs.

'Gavin, please,' said Mum, opening the window.

And the funny thing was, it was only after Mum opened the window that I could smell the sick and the poo.

'Why do they call it cold turkey?' I asked.

'I don't know, my darling, but it's not quite right because sometimes you're hot and sometimes you're cold and sometimes it's both at the same time. But I've never puked so much in my life. I couldn't believe there was that much crap in me. And then, at the end of it all, they make you clean up your room by yourself, when you are so weak you can barely lift a finger. That's not much fun, is it?'

'No!' I said.

Someone knocked at the door, not waiting for us to answer before coming in. He was a tall man wearing jeans, a brown jumper and plimsolls. He looked just like all the people that used to visit our flat late at night. He probably was one of them – there were so many towards the end. But he was someone important now; he was a therapist.

'Hey, man,' said Dad.

'Hey, man. So this is your gang, I've heard so much about you all. I'm Jeff,' he said.

He looked at us, and when he saw me, he looked even harder.

'I think we have a session now. Which is great.'

I had to have therapy too. Mum had already explained this. She told me it was important. She didn't want me repeating patterns, learning behaviour, holding on to negative emotions.

'Good luck!' said Dad.

I didn't want to go with Jeff.

'How about here,' said Jeff once we'd walked so far away from the building, across grass and under trees, that there was no way Mum and Dad would have been able to hear me if I'd shouted for them.

'OK,' I said. I dropped to the ground, crossing my legs and patting my skirt down so he wouldn't be able to see my pants.

'So, how old are you?'

'I just turned nine.'

'Happy birthday!'

'Thanks.'

The ground was damp and it was too cold to be sitting outside like this.

'So, do you know why you are here?'

'Yes.'

'And do you know why your father is here?'

'Because he doesn't want to be a heroin addict any more.'

Jeff sighed as though I'd said something stupid. This annoyed me because I knew that I was not stupid.

'Your dad will be an addict until the day he dies. This disease doesn't just disappear because you do the programme. It is like cancer, you know. You never really recover from cancer, there is always a chance it will come back, if you're not careful.'

I looked at the grass, felt it beneath my hand; there were whole civilizations of bugs and worms down there. I loved lawns, loved grass. Sometimes I would go to Battersea Park by myself just so I could lie on the grass.

'Right,' said Jeff. 'Let's get started.'

He opened his folder, letting some documents fall to the ground, finding what he was looking for. He crossed his legs and held a piece of paper, reading from it as if this was the first time he had ever seen it.

'Can you remember when you first became aware that your dad was using?'

Creeping into the sitting room late at night, the sweet smell of cooking heroin, balls of rolled-up silver foil, beige powder and money being handed over. This has been happening all my life.

'No.'

'OK,' said Jeff. He paused before he asked the next question.

'Does your dad often break promises?'

Dad has promised to take me to the zoo. It is a Sunday morning. The time pulses away on the LED displays of the video recorders – we have VHS and Betamax. I am ready, coat on, shoes on, breakfast eaten. I sit on the sofa waiting. Every so often I go to his bedroom door, stand outside, say 'Dad' softly. I know he must be tired but it is getting late and we are meant to be going to the zoo, not the little one in Battersea Park, but the big one in Regent's Park. Someone told me that there was a huge cage with monkeys in it, loads of them, and that they swing about and groom each other just like they do on the TV.

'Dad,' I whisper.

Then I say it louder, and louder again. I am getting annoyed. I really want to go to the zoo and he promised.

I push open the door, walk into the sweaty, shadowy room. The bed is a mattress on the floor; the duvet is knotted around his legs.

'Dad,' I say, walking towards him. He is just in his pants and there is white scum at the corners of his mouth. He is holding his head with both hands.

'My head, it is broken, it is broken in half, my head,' he says, and I realize that he is trying to hold his head together with his hands, to stop his brains spilling out all over the pillow. I run to him, kneel next to him. I daren't touch him, but I look closely.

'Dad, are you OK, do you need a doctor?'

I can't see blood or bone or brain. I can't see the bit where his head is broken.

'My head is broken in two,' he goes on, as though he hasn't heard me, as though he doesn't know that I am there. And I realize that he hasn't heard me, that he doesn't know I am there, and that his head is not broken.

I walk out. I close the door. I take off my coat.

'Does your dad often break promises?'

'No.'

Jeff looked through his papers, twiddling his blue biro.

'You really don't want to talk, do you?' he said eventually.

This time I didn't even reply. So he would get the message.

'OK. Let's try something different.' Jeff handed me a packet of used felt-tip pens, a piece of plain A4 paper and a clipboard. 'Draw a picture, anything you like. It would be great if it had something to do with how you feel about your dad's using, but it doesn't matter if it doesn't, just draw whatever you fancy, whatever comes to mind.'

'And what are you going to do?' I asked.

'I'm going to smoke a cigarette,' he said, getting out a packet of Rothmans, lighting one, lying on his back and blowing smoke up into the low, grey sky.

I was not very good at drawing, but I decided to give

it a go so that I would have something to show Mum. It was tricky. I was better at the building than the people. It took me a long time, but in the end I was pleased with what I'd done. It sort of looked like I wanted it to.

Jeff had conked out.

I poked him with a pen. 'I've finished,' I said.

'OK, great, right,' he said, flustered, trying to pretend he hadn't been asleep.

I handed him the piece of paper. He looked at it for a moment, squinting to show that he was concentrating.

'So, this is you, right, sitting outside the pub, and the two people we can see inside, the two heads, these are your parents?'

'That's right,' I said.

'And did this happen to you often, them going to the pub and leaving you outside?'

'All the time.'

'That must have been really tough. And did they get very drunk when they were in the pub?'

'Yes, very.'

'And how did all this make you feel?'

I paused, had a think. How did this make me feel?

'Upset, I suppose, sad, lonely, afraid, all those sorts of things.'

'This is really good, Amanda. It's really good to talk like this; you'll feel so much better for it, I promise. So, back to the pub. Can you remember the first time this happened?'

I didn't tell him that my name was not Amanda.

*

Jeff let me take the drawing. I handed it to Mum and Dad as if it was a prize certificate. They looked at it, standing next to each other in the entrance area. It was nearly time to go.

'But this never happened,' said Mum. 'We never left you sitting outside the pub.'

'I know!' I said.

Dad was the first one to see the joke. I knew he would get it. That was why I had done it.

'You little tinker!' he said, laughing.

Then Mum got it too and laughed for the first time in months. And we were all happy, in that place, laughing about the thing that never happened, laughing because I had tricked Jeff, laughing because at least it wasn't bad in that way. It was bad in ways that I didn't know how to say, how to draw, how to write.

7

2014, Yorkshire

I have booked myself on to a week-long course called 'Writing for Children and Young Adults'. I want to finish the novel I have been working on. It is about a troubled teenaged girl whose mother is a high-class prostitute, whose father is mentally disturbed and who has magic powers that enable her to harness the conscious energy of the universe. In one scene an ancient being takes her on a mind-bending journey to the moon. The book is quite good, I think, if a little niche.

I'm anxious on the journey north to Hebden Bridge. I'm leaving my children for the first time since Minna was born. Every train I'm meant to catch is cancelled, my subconscious fears somehow impacting the physical world. But I'm happy when I finally arrive and am shown my pretty first-floor room overlooking fields and forests. I unpack and arrange all my stationery and cosmetics in neat lines on the desk and the dressing table before going downstairs for 'welcome cake'. The other students are mostly middle-aged women, many of them teachers, most of whom have done these sorts of courses many times before. We gather in a little room crammed with too many chairs, our cups of tea and plates of cake balanced on our knees. I wedge myself into a corner and watch, not speaking.

I feel less self-conscious that evening, after dinner and a couple of glasses of wine. We are in the barn next to the main house. Sofas are arranged in a large semi-circle. We all have our notebooks and pens. One of the teachers asks us to write about something that happened to us when we were young.

'Really think about how you felt in your body, transport yourself back to that time,' she says.

I begin to write, really trying to transport myself, really trying to feel it in my body.

I write about visiting my dad when he was in a rehabilitation centre. I try to remember how it felt to be that girl, so excited to see her dad, so anxious about her mum, trying to hold them all together, but never quite managing it. As I write I find that there is so much that I can recall. Details from the past pop into my mind as though I have summoned them: the blackboard with Dad's name written in chalk letters, the sugar crumble texture of the chocolate biscuit, the cold grass against my skin during the session with Jeff.

It's like going back in time. It's like magic.

I close my notebook. My breath is coming fast. The other students share what they have written. I do not.

The next morning, in my room overlooking fields and forests, I reread what I have written. I like it. I think it might even be better than the story about the girl who travels to the moon. But there is something about this evocation of my past that bothers me.

Where is Candy? She would have been about four when Dad went into rehab, and would surely have come with us to the centre. The act of writing has allowed my mind to retrieve so much. But not Candy.

So I try again. I try to write the story with her in it, imagining the three of us on the train, me making it fun for Candy by telling her that we were going to the sea-side, us in the back of the cab singing along to the music on the radio, Dad hugging all three of us to him, his girls, me fetching Candy chocolate bourbons from the biscuit tin, her bouncing on Dad's single bed as I go for my session. I make the story as rich and detailed as I can.

I know even as I am doing it that I am making it up, inventing her and inventing myself in relation to her. The invention feels flimsy, as if she is made of air, without weight, not even a ghost.

But surely if I keep going, if I keep looking, keep summoning that magic, I will be able to find Candy again. If I can sort my past into cool, dispassionate, descriptive sentences, she will be there, hiding in the gaps, the white spaces.

People only hide because they think they will be found.

I don't need to see a therapist, I decide, I can just do this instead. I set aside my fantasy novel and start writing stories about my past.

I write about junkies and smoky rooms and overfull ashtrays and feeling alone even when my parents are with me. I write about swimming pools and broken tables and sweet squirty cream. I remember how things tasted, smelt, felt. I remember my eyes wide and my heart fast as I watched it all and tried to work it out: what should I be doing, where is the danger? I remember my mother, slumped and sad; my father, jittery and bug-eyed, always with an excuse, a joke. I remember the porn mags, the violent films. I remember seeing things that I did not understand. I do not remember Candy, but I do remember fear.

I try to write elegant, controlled prose that will some-how make all these memories manageable.

As the week progresses I begin to feel strange, anx-ious and dislocated, my mind churning with difficult emotions. Memories rear up out of the darkness. Writ-ing these things down hasn't made them safe, it hasn't contained them – quite the opposite, it's given them a life of their own. At night I lie in my small room over-looking dark woods and I cannot sleep. I feel tired and yet full of adrenaline. I feel as if I am thinning out, because now part of me is in the past, a place I have worked so hard to escape, running and running and not looking back.

The feeling does not pass when I get back to London. I am a stranger when I walk into my home and hug my children, who jump and shout, so excited to see me, and my husband who holds me close. Who are these people? How did I get here?

This is what thinking about the past has done to me.

And yet I still write.

Every day on the train to work I write about my child-hood, my broken family, the things that happened before Candy died, the things that happened after she died, circling round, trying to find a lost girl in all the madness that I don't seem able to put in order even though I write and I write. On Saturday mornings I sit in a café with my laptop and type up all that I have written during the week. I walk home, to my husband, to my children, in a daze, my body in the present, my brain in the past, my heart who knows where.

8

1989, London

On my first day back at school after the holiday in Tunisia I was so happy. I felt light as I skipped down the stairs, away from our flat, where Candy's suitcase still stood unpacked in her unchanged bedroom, with the teddies arranged in rows and naked Barbies having a barbecue in their pink plastic condo. I wore my new shoes and carried my new bag. Mum and Dad had gone mad buying me new things. 'You're an only child now, so we can spoil you,' they said as if this was some sort of silver lining.

I stood at the bus stop and listened to *Hounds of Love* by Kate Bush on my new yellow waterproof Sony Walkman. It was my first day, but everyone else had gone back yesterday. I'd stayed at home so that an announcement could be made without me. This was something that had been decided by Mum and the headmistress. One day away from school so that I would not have to be there when Mrs Rudland made her speech.

'I have some sad news, pupils,' she would begin, and their ears would prick up; they would wriggle with anticipation, sitting cross-legged on the golden polished parquet. 'I am sorry to inform you that Gavanndra Hodge's younger sister died very suddenly on holiday during the Easter break. Candida died of a virus which is not contagious. Can we please do our best to help Gavanndra during this difficult time.'

There would be a communal gasp, a ripple of whispers, five hundred heads turning to see if they could see her, the girl whose sister had died suddenly, on holiday of all places.

I was glad I didn't have to be there for that bit, for the moment when they all turned to look at me.

I got off the Tube and walked towards school.

Cars blocked the road, mothers honked their horns, girls in short grey skirts and black loafers gathered at the entrance shrieking, hugging, kissing.

Venetia had shiny golden hair and shiny tanned legs and ran across the road, not checking for traffic. She grabbed my arm with both hands and started talking. 'Cammy has a new boyfriend and we're going to meet him at McDonald's after school. But my mum has told me only to eat chips, because she doesn't want me to get mad cow disease. How are you?'

'I'm . . .'

I can't move. I can't breathe. I can't stop watching.

'I'm fine.'

She pulled me into the dark muddle of the cloakrooms, where all the loos seemed to be flushing at once. We walked up the stairs to our form room. There were jumpers and bags slung across the carpet-tiled floor; everyone was sitting on their desks chatting. 'Hi,' a couple of people said.

'Can everyone please sit down and be quiet for register!' shouted our form mistress.

Miss Von Haniel nodded at me when I answered 'yes' to my name, but didn't smile or make a sad face or anything. Then we all traipsed down the stairs to the assembly hall and it was like the noise of an incoming army, all the heavy black-soled shoes on the wooden steps. Nothing seemed different. There were girls with bad acne, girls with nice hair, the handsome new English teacher who looked like something from a Merchant Ivory film. Anya walked up right behind him, so close that they were virtually touching. She pretended to bump into the back of him and I was laughing so hard that I was still giggling by the time we had to sit down, cross-legged, on the floor.

'Good morning, everyone,' said Mrs Rudland from the stage at the front of the hall. Her glasses were so thick they made her eyes look double the size. 'This morning we are very lucky because Maggie Chan is going to give us a short clarinet recital.'

Anya pinched my arm and rolled her eyes and Venetia groaned and we leant on each other and pretended to go to sleep because we were so bored by the clarinet recital.

At break, after morning lessons, I bought myself a packet of Skips and a cup of tea. I blew on my tea to cool it and laid a Skip on my tongue and enjoyed the fizzy feeling of it dissolving. Priti had a bandage on her hand.

'I was trying to give myself a tattoo,' she said.

'Damaris has a tattoo,' said Sarah, staring over my shoulder.

We all turned to look. Damaris was a sixth-former with dyed black hair down to her bottom and perfectly applied black liquid eyeliner. She was wearing a leather biker jacket, a packet of Marlboro Reds hanging from one pocket. She looked like the sort of person who could handle anything that happened to her.

'It's a dolphin, on her ankle,' said Sarah.

'You fancy her, you lesbian,' said Venetia.

'I fancy her too,' said Priti.

'I want to be her,' I said.

'You're all lesbians,' said Venetia.

After break I had Latin. Our teacher was Miss Yeats, who was very small with painted-on eyebrows so she always looked supercilious (*super* meaning above, *cilium* meaning eyelid, therefore, *supercilium*, eyebrow). Her skirt was so long that I couldn't see her feet, so it looked as though she was moving around on rollers. She rolled to her desk and picked up a pile of burgundy work books, and then rolled around, throwing them at us. Before any of us were allowed to sit down we each had to get a bit of vocab right.

'*Aquila.*'

'Eagle.'

'Sit down.'

We talked about *The Aeneid* Book Two. We talked about a city crashing to the ground in a hot country far away, death all around, horror and blood and implacable gods who watch people suffering and do nothing to help. For some reason people think it is OK to talk about these things just because they happened a long time ago and Virgil has arranged them into neat lines. But it doesn't seem OK to me. Two thousand years is nothing and poetry just makes things scarier ('ut tandem ante oculus evasit et ora parentum/concidit ac multo vitam cum sanguine fudit', meaning 'and then his parents saw him and he fell to the ground dead, his life flowing out of him with much blood.')

In the dining hall at lunch we packed ourselves around a narrow table to eat lasagne, chips and salad and drink tap water out of ridged plastic cups. Venetia told us that her brother had worked out how to get high inhaling Tipp-Ex thinner, but no one had any Tipp-Ex thinner so we couldn't try it.

'Look at Jane,' Anya whispered while the others were talking.

Jane was in the year above. Her father had been a famous television actor. He had died suddenly. We all knew about that; it had been on the news, in the papers. He had died years ago, but ten years ago is nothing and over the holidays she had lost too much weight so that now she was just bare bones really, her cheekbones protruding, the sinews in her neck straining, her hair mostly fallen out and the few dry strands that remained backcombed and teased into a bun on the top of her head to give the impression of density where there was none.

I couldn't help but stare, although I looked away when Jane caught my eye.

'What is she doing in here anyway?' said Venetia.

'She probably just wants to smell the food,' said Sarah, and we all laughed.

I had chemistry after lunch. No one mucked about in chemistry: we were dealing with dangerous chemicals, acids that could burn and metals that could explode; but

73

if they were contained, if they were kept behind glass, they could be controlled, lithium in a test tube, all that wild intensity made safe.

'So whose house shall we get ready at?' said Sarah.

We were sitting around a speckled Formica table in McDonald's. I had a strawberry milkshake and some French fries. Anna was smoking, flicking the ash into the foil ashtray. The rumour was that she had already lost her virginity.

'Mine,' I said.

They were quiet. They looked at each other.

'What, you're coming to the ball?' said Anya.

'Yeah,' I said. 'My dad can drive us.'

'Cool,' said Venetia.

At home Mum was sitting on the sofa.

'How was it? Were they kind, your teachers? Was everyone kind?'

She had come home early from the model agency in Covent Garden where she now worked as an accountant on this, my first day back at school, to make sure I was all right.

'It was fine,' I said, throwing my school bag into my bedroom, my bag which was full of new textbooks, the comforting weight of normal life resumed.

'I had Latin and chemistry today, so that was great.'

'OK,' Mum said. 'That sounds . . . good. But, you know, were they kind, your teachers?'

'Yes, they were kind,' I said and walked away from her

into the kitchen. I didn't tell her that they had been so very kind that no one had mentioned Candy, that five hundred people had spent all day acting as though this momentous, terrible thing that had happened to us hadn't actually happened at all.

No one wanted me to talk about my dead sister; no one wanted me to have a dead sister. They wanted me to pretend my sister hadn't died, and in order to do that I had to pretend that my sister had never lived.

So that is what I would do.

'Oh, by the way, everyone's going to come round here to get ready for the ball next week,' I shouted from the kitchen. 'Dad can drive us.'

'You're going to the ball?'

'I don't want to waste the ticket.'

'You mustn't worry about that.'

I walked from the kitchen, went to stand in front of her, tried to look purposeful.

'I want to go.'

Dad let us drink cans of beer in the car on the way to the Hammersmith Palais; even though we'd already finished a bottle of white wine at home. He let us smoke too, so that when we drew up outside the Hammersmith Palais, sunglasses on, fags and beer, we felt like the coolest kids there. Venetia had a flask of whisky that she'd tucked into the top of her tights, and we went straight to the loos so we could drink it and put on more lipstick, more powder, our spots hidden under layers of greasy cover-up, stripes of blusher on our cheeks, our eyelashes clagged with black mascara.

We walked out into the heat and music.

'Don't You Want Me' by The Human League was playing.

The floor was a damp black carpet, the ceilings were low, the walls were black and sweating. There were sofas in the corners writhing with bodies, boys and girls, the boys in black tie, their shirts untucked, their bow ties lost; the girls in watered silk and crushed velvet, their netting underskirts pushed up to reveal stockings into which were tucked packets of cigarettes and ten-pound notes. The boys lay on top of the girls, between their legs, their faces were pressed together, their jaws moving, their eyes closed, hands roving, as though it was all so urgent and important. As we moved around the edge of the dance floor, a shadowy place where there were more of these sofas, so many more of these bodies, I saw a pack of boys steal the money from a girl's stocking; then I saw a girl on top of a boy, her legs astride him, covering his lap with red taffeta, and she was sitting up and he was lying back and they both had their eyes closed and were moving hardly at all, just the occasional jerking motion. They're actually having sex, I thought. A schoolboy materialized out of the darkness and took Anya's hand, led her to one of the sofas, then the same thing happened to Sarah, to Venetia, and finally to me. I didn't really see his face or ask his name – those things didn't matter. But he did have a can of Coke that smelt like rum, which he offered to me and I drank before we kissed.

And this felt better, this blurry intensity, this way of trying to forget: alcohol and music and boys; this was it.

9

2014, London

It is a Monday morning at work and we are having the weekly meeting in which we go through the forthcoming features for the magazine, the entire editorial staff squeezed into Kate's office. During the meeting my phone rings. It is my mother. I decline the call but I feel agitated as the meeting proceeds, assuming something is wrong and wondering what it is. As soon as the meeting is over, I call her.

'Hi, Mum!'
  'Hello?'
  She sounds distant and confused.
  'Mum, hello, are you OK?'
  My mother lives in sheltered accommodation in Norwood Junction. She has type 2 diabetes, has lost most of the sensation in the soles of her feet and has injections in her eyes every couple of months to stop her from going blind. She is a deacon at the local Baptist church, a modern building where I watched her being submerged in tepid water for her rebaptism. She enjoys singing in the church choir and ordering random gizmos from QVC that clutter her small, over-heated flat.

She collects my children from school two days a week, on Tuesdays and Thursdays, and looks after them until I get home from work.

'I feel dizzy, I think . . . I can't breathe.'

My mother has some sores on her leg that she has been treating with sugar and manuka honey. Every time I have seen her lately I have asked how they are getting on; wounds take a long time to heal when you are a diabetic. She keeps saying that the bites are getting much better, even though I can see them weeping pus through the dressings.

'I'm calling an ambulance,' I say.

The ambulance is on its way. I call Mum to let her know and tell her that I will meet her in the hospital. I call her accommodation manager and ask her to sit with Mum until the ambulance arrives. Twenty minutes later she calls me to say that the ambulance is taking Mum to the hospital.

I call the childminder who looks after the girls on Mondays and Wednesdays and ask if she can cover for Mum this week. I fizz with organizational energy. I am good in a crisis, fast-moving and unemotional. When the apocalypse comes I will be in my element.

I phone the emergency services. 'Hello, you have my mother in an ambulance, could you tell me which hospital you are taking her to, please?'

'What's your mother's name?'

'Jan Hodge. You just collected her.'

'No, sorry, we have no record of that.'

'But you just collected her.'

'Call back in twenty minutes. The system might have been updated by then.'

I try to do some work, but I find that I can't concentrate. My mother is the only other person left in the world who really knew Candy, but now she is in an ambulance somewhere in South London and I cannot find her. I phone the ambulance service again and again. After an hour they are able to locate her.

'Ah yes, she is at Lewisham.'

I get a cab there and find Mum in a wheelchair in the waiting room. She seems so old and disorientated. I buy her a tea and she holds it loosely in her elegant hands, too exhausted to lift the polystyrene cup to her lips.

Eventually we are seen by a young female doctor. She talks to my mum about the sores on her legs and how long she has had them. Mum tells the doctor about the anti-bacterial properties of manuka honey. The doctor asks my mother to lie on a bed and starts to unwrap the bandages. I hear the doctor gasp and I can suddenly smell the rotten tang of pus.

'You really should have gone to your GP with this,' the doctor says. She almost sounds angry.

Mum, it transpires, has cellulitis and sepsis. She is admitted to hospital and put on an antibiotic drip. I promise to collect some things – a nightie, her Kindle – and bring them to her.

I feel shaky as I walk to the bus stop. I can't stop thinking about how my mother looked in her wheelchair, so weak and diminished. I can still smell the stench of her wounds. What is wrong with me? Normally I am so good at this stuff. I am like a robot in an emergency. Don't feel, don't think, just act. It is how I have survived, again and again. More than once my husband has said that he wishes I would cry now and again, show some emotion. When he says this I get defensive, but really I am thinking I cannot start crying, because how would I stop?

I wipe the unexpected, unbidden, unwelcome tears from my face and get on the bus, but still they fall.

My mother is in hospital for a week, slipping in and out of consciousness, hallucinating that the tall, swaying trees outside the windows are whispering secrets to her. She doesn't tell the doctors about these hallucinations; she worries that if she does the doctors will keep her in hospital longer and she won't be able to return home, to her life, to us. Just as I do not tell anyone about my tears. We keep our vulnerabilities to ourselves.

10

1989, London

It was cream and brown, mostly fur. Its bones were tiny. I could feel them as I held it on my knee, a quivery, shivery creature, its warm heartbeat too fast against my fingertips.

'I'm going to call it Dizzy,' I said. 'After Dizzy Gillespie.'

It was one of the smallest rabbits in the garden. I had spotted it at once, bouncing towards me rather than away from me, as though it wanted to be mine.

'How old do you think it is?' I asked.

'I don't know,' said Bella.

She was on her knees by one of the hutches, pulling wads of pale straw from a big plastic bag; shoving the fresh straw into the hutch without clearing out the old, damp, flattened straw. She had copper ringlets and she wore a black Lycra miniskirt, a white vest and sandals that were scuffed and brown, like her bare legs.

The rabbit garden was around the corner from Bella's house in Chelsea. It was attached to a block of flats that her father was renting out and he had loaned the garden to Bella for her pet rabbits. The garden had a black metal gate that creaked on its hinges and a huge ash tree which shaded it. At first there had only been four rabbits, but they had multiplied fast. Now they were in piles in the corners and nestled among the roots of the tree. Old fat ones sat slowly munching blackened carrot stumps; small new ones darted about what little space there was, scampering over the backs of their parents, aunts, uncles, their velvet ears flapping. I had to nudge them out of the way with my toes to get to the bentwood chair under the tree.

'How many are there now?'

'Don't ask. I hate them. They arc such randy little shits,' she lisped. Bella shuffled next to me on the seat, late September sunlight warming us through the branches and leaves. She grabbed one of the biggest, oldest rabbits, yellowish white with scummy pink eyes. 'But I don't hate you, oh no I don't, I love you,' she said, holding the rabbit's face to hers, then draping it over her shoulders like an expensive stole.

'What are you going to do about them?'

'Don't you start. The people in the flats have been complaining. They say they can smell them, but it takes so long to clean the bloody hutches. Dad says we should start eating them.'

'*Lapin à la moutarde*,' I said, remembering something I'd seen on a sign outside a restaurant on a school day-trip to Boulogne.

'I'll kill him before I let him kill any of them.'

'Well, I'm taking Dizzy, so that's one less rabbit for dinner.'

Bella gave me a hutch and a bag of hay. Her mother

drove me home over the river in her green Morris Minor, which had moss growing on the wooden interior panels. I held Dizzy on my lap, even though they both said I should keep him in the hutch for the journey.

I hadn't told my parents I was getting a rabbit.

'You can't keep a rabbit in your bedroom,' Dad said.

'Yes, I can,' I said. I had already set up the hutch; Dizzy was inside, comfortable in the hay. I had put in some fresh lettuce leaves and a carrot but he hadn't eaten any-thing yet. 'Anyway, Mum says it's fine.'

Dizzy was a very cute baby rabbit with curiously human tendencies. I discovered that he didn't really like raw vegetables, he much preferred buttery toast and double cream. He would bounce around the flat as though he was in a field, gaily cocking his white fluffy bottom, leaving sticky raisin droppings all over the carpet. He liked to sit with me in front of the television, watching *Neighbours* and *Home and Away*. One time I came home from school to find my mother with the rabbit on her lap, singing to it. Mum began to feed the rabbit, preparing dainty snacks for it, steamed asparagus and tender-stem broccoli. She took over the job of cleaning the hutch, taking a dustpan and brush to it, making sure the hay was always plentiful and fresh, so that Dizzy would have a soft, scented bed to sleep on at night.

'Your mum thinks that rabbit is Candy reincarnated,' said Dad.

Candy had been dead for less than six months.

'She has come back to us,' Mum said.

Dizzy kept growing. When I'd first brought him home

he was small enough to sit on my palm. By Christmas he was nearly as long as my thigh. We let him on to the table and tried to fix a paper crown to his head. We fed him chipolatas wrapped in bacon and dipped in gravy. But his favourite thing, we discovered, was brandy butter. He licked the plastic container clean. The following week my mother bought tubs of discounted brandy butter from Marks & Spencer and kept them in the freezer for Dizzy, to be defrosted and fed to him as a special weekend treat. She liked to eat them too.

Dizzy kept growing (and so did Mum).

He was getting too big for his hutch, but still I put him in every night before I went to bed. One night I was woken by the sound of him kicking at the wooden door, a sinister thudding noise. Two days later he kicked so hard that he broke it.

'He's a monster,' Dad said.

'He's just growing up,' said Mum, looking sad.

Spottynose never liked Dizzy. She was a clever cat. She slept at the end of my bed, checked my hair for fleas and always sat with me if I was sad. When we came home from the holiday in Tunisia, she looked at us, three instead of four, sniffed the air and pattered straight into Candy's room. She did not come out for two days.

I came home from school to discover that Dizzy had once again kicked his way out of his hutch, even though we had fixed it. He was roaming around the house like a restless hoodlum. Spottynose had wedged herself under a radiator, the fur on her belly chewed away.

'Maybe we shouldn't have given him the chipolatas,' said Dad.

'I don't think we can keep him any more,' I said.

I had become scared of Dizzy.

My mother cried.

Bella's mother drove back over the river to collect the rabbit. Bella told me that she had found a lovely family in Somerset who would take him.

'They have two young children who really want a big rabbit like this. They have a massive garden; he'll be so happy. He'll be loved.'

That made me and Mum feel a bit better.

A month later Bella's rabbit garden was cleared out. It had become impossible, unmanageable, with dead rabbits decaying in the roots of the trees.

Years later I spoke to her about the rabbits.

'What did you do with them?' I asked.

'We packed as many as we could into the boot of the car,' she said, her lisp now gone, her copper ringlets blonde and straight. 'We had to really shove them in. It was mayhem. Then we drove down to Kent, found a field and let them out. It took three trips.'

'Wow,' I said, thinking that Dizzy was lucky to get out when he did. Those rabbits wouldn't have survived a day in the wild. 'And did you ever hear from the family who took my rabbit? Were they happy with him? He was a bit of a nutter, but cute. He loved brandy butter.'

'Oh, Gavvy. There was no family. I'm sorry.'

11

2014, London

The Duke of Marlborough has died. This is a big story at *Tatler.* Sonny Marlborough was wealthy, much-married and the owner of Blenheim Palace, England's very own Versailles. But even more thrilling to the team is his son, Jamie Blandford, former degenerate drug addict, now apparently reformed and about to take his place as one of the most senior aristocrats of England. Also a former client and friend of my father's.

The editorial team know that Jamie was a 'family friend', so it is agreed that I should be the one to contact him and ask if he would like to be interviewed by *Tatler.* It would be quite a coup, although I make clear that I don't think I could do the interview (and I very much doubt he would want to be interviewed by me).

I write a commiserating letter. I wait a week for the reply that doesn't come, and then find Jamie on Facebook. I send him a personal message. He replies with his mobile phone number and we arrange a time to speak.

Just hearing his voice makes me feel strange. But I have to be grown-up and polite. He asks how I am. I tell him that I'm now married and have two children. He asks their names, their ages, and then he laughs. 'How funny! I have a child who is the same age as yours.' He says it as though this is an amusing coincidence.

'How funny,' I say.

I make an excuse to end the conversation.

I knew Jamie had remarried. But the idea that he should be in charge of a child, this man who took drugs in my house when I was a little girl, makes me feel helpless and sad in a way that I could not have predicted.

The new Duke of Marlborough declines the opportunity to be interviewed by *Tatler*. Instead, one of the journalists on the magazine, David Jenkins, writes a profile of him, one that portrays Jamie's past shortcomings as well as his recent rehabilitation. I help by putting David in touch with some of Jamie (and Dad's) old friends, like Michael, whom I meet in the gilt VIP bar of the Café Royal hotel where he is employed as a 'host'. Michael is still handsome, louche in his purple suit, his blond hair gone to grey. He is with some acquaintances, glossy young people who find him entertaining, a living slice of decadent London history. He introduces me.

'This is Gavanndra. Her father was my drug dealer!'

How they laugh.

'I first met Gavin when I was, what, sixteen? On exeat. That's right, isn't it?'

'I don't know. I wasn't there for that bit,' I say.

Michael laughs, laughter that morphs into a phlegmy cough. He will be dead from liver cancer within the year.

I thought they were his friends. But what I realize as I sit there, listening to Michael shouting over party music, drinking my complimentary vodka and tonic too fast and asking for another, is that to most of these people Dad was just a drug dealer. And here am I, deputy editor of their magazine, the daughter of their drug dealer.

I don't know if the joke is on them or me.

The next day I tell David about Jamie coming to our flat when I was young, how I would watch him take drugs and find him asleep on the floor of our living room the next morning. I do not tell David about the last time I saw Jamie. We were in Dad's basement hairdressing salon in Knightsbridge. It was late. I was there with some school friends, drinking, smoking, getting high. Jamie tramped down the stairs.

'Hello! Would anyone like some crack?' he said.

Perhaps he was joking, perhaps not. Either way, Jamie and Dad went to the back room, the place where the hair colours were mixed, where powdered blue bleach filled the air like a sour dust cloud and where clandestine transactions took place.

David has finished writing his piece about Jamie. The picture editor has chosen the images, the designer has laid out the story, and it lands on my desk so that I can come up with the headline. There is a huge image of Jamie on the opening spread, at the age he would have been when I knew him, sweaty and wild-eyed.

My past is crashing into the present with ever-increasing violence and it is all I can do to keep standing.

12

1990, London

I would smoke in bed when I couldn't sleep, drink strong coffee and listen to Dad's old records played very quietly, Jimi Hendrix and Janis Joplin, watching the brightness move on the ceiling, patterns made by the cars' headlights on the road outside.

One night when I was lying there I heard a black cab pulling up outside, and then Dad's voice. I listened to him, stumbling up the stairs, struggling to get his key in the lock, slamming the door, humming loudly, not caring that everyone was meant to be asleep.

Usually I would just lie there as he weaved his way drunkenly about the flat, knocking things over and giggling, but that night some old instinct made me get up and go to him, even though it was late and I had school the next day.

He wasn't where I expected to find him, beached on the sofa, the ashtray balanced on his belly, his feet on the pouffe, buckle of his jeans undone.

Where was he?

Then I spotted him sitting on the arm of the chair by the open window, blowing thick smoke into the night.

'Bloody hell!' he said, coughing when he saw me.

The cigarette he was smoking was not a normal one – I noticed that at once; it was homemade, a roll-up, the smoke smelt different too.

'What's that?' I asked.

Dad smiled his wolf smile and took another drag. The cold air from the communal gardens where we used to play, trees and grass and icy black sky, made me shiver as I stood there, barefoot in my nightie.

'It's just dope, my darling,' he said. 'Nothing to worry about.'

I took a step closer. Dad was taking drugs again. This should have scared me, but it didn't. I was numb to everything. 'Does Mum know?' I asked.

Dad looked at me; his eyes were laughing as though he didn't care. 'It really doesn't matter, it's nothing, it's not my drug of choice.'

I watched Dad's hands as he flicked ash on to the window ledge. It would be blown away in the night, I thought. No one would ever know, I thought.

'Is it nice?' I asked. I don't know why. The question just popped into my brain.

He looked at me. 'Have you done any drugs yet?'

We are in Anya's bedroom in Chiswick, sitting on the carpet, our grey skirts so tight and short it is hard to cross our legs.

'Do you think we need one each?' asks Anya, holding up a big peach-coloured towel that she has just fetched from her bathroom.

'We haven't got any contagious diseases, have we? Let's share,' says Sarah.

Anya sits down, crosses her legs, lays the towel over her knees and reads the instructions on the side of the can of deodorant, as though they might be helpful at all.

'So . . . what do we do?'

'Just hold the towel over your mouth and spray, inhale, repeat,' says Venetia.

Anya holds the towel to her face, brings the deodorant to her mouth and presses the nozzle, keeping her eyes open. It makes a loud, fizzy noise. She stops, smiles, says, 'Ooh, it tastes weird!' and presses again, inhaling for about ten seconds, her eyes closed. She makes a choking, giggly sound and falls back, so that now she is lying on the carpet, her legs still crossed.

'Was that meant to happen?' whispers Sarah.

And then Anya opens her eyes and begins laughing, still lying on her back. 'Oh my God! That was amazing!'

'Me next,' I say. I hold the towel to my face and push the nozzle down with my finger. The chalky taste of Natrel deodorant fills my mouth, but I keep going, breathing in the fumes until my hands are weak, like rubber, and curtains are coming down on my mind, blackness and a whomp-whomping sound in my ears, which is like the sound of my heart, but only if my heart was huge, and in my head, and my head was the size of a football pitch, and the blackness is infinite and I am floating in it and everything feels soft and amazing and there is no one except me.

The sounds fade and the black becomes grey and suddenly I am in the room again, lying on my back. It takes a moment to work out what just happened, I don't know how long I was gone, thirty seconds or thirty years. I start laughing; I can't help it. The laughter starts in my belly and bubbles up and out. Everything is just so funny and brilliant; it is impossible to suppress how happy I feel.

'Yeah,' I said.

Dad stared out at the night, the joint crackling between his fingers.

'Do you want some?' he said, reaching out his hand.

'Yeah,' I said.

I took the joint from him. I brought it to my lips; the end was thin and wet from his mouth. It was hard to take a drag, but I sucked hard and eventually the end glowed and I felt the sharp, dry fumes slide down my throat into my lungs.

'Hold it for as long as possible,' he said, but I thought I might choke so I coughed out the smoke and he laughed.

The effect wasn't as instant and overwhelming as the aerosol, but it made my brain nicely heavy and my body feel as if it was swaying even though I was sure I was standing still. I took another drag, wanting to be sure of the sensation. It was easier the second time, now I knew what I was doing, easier to hold the smoke down, to blow it out smoothly rather than cough it up.

I handed the joint back and Dad chucked it out of the window. I felt my legs go soft so I sat down.

'It's nice stuff, probably stronger than you're used to,' he murmured.

'Mmmm,' I replied, interested by how my lips felt against one another; they sort of buzzed.

'You should come to me, you know, when you want to get stuff. I mean, I know you're gonna do it, so this way it's safer. Who knows what you'll get out on the street, rat poison and all sorts of crap. But if you get it from me it will be good, and I'll know what you are taking. Much safer.'

I felt dizzy and a little sick, my thoughts going around in circles. Dad was telling me that he would get drugs for me, if I wanted them.

'That would be cool,' I said and he reached into his jeans pocket and took out a lump of black stuff wrapped in cellophane. He unwound the plastic, broke off an edge and handed it to me.

'Here,' he said.

The hash was soft and warm. I held it tightly in my fist.

'Don't tell Mum about this. She wouldn't get it.'

'I won't.'

'Come on, bedtime,' he said and he shut the window.

As he left the living room he patted the wooden box on the mantelpiece.

'Night night, Candy,' he said.

13

2014, London

I know all about how to deal with emotional pain. The methods I know, the ones I learnt as a young woman, they don't stop the tears, but they do stop you feeling the tears, so you can just wipe them away and start laughing again.

That's what Dad would want. Not this morose introspection, not this sitting in drab South London cafés drinking cold tea and tap-tap-tapping away on a computer, lost in the past. 'Who cares about yesterday, how about right fucking now?' That's what Dad would say. That is what he does say, when I make him speak inside my head. 'Candy and me, we're having a laugh up here. You're the one we're worried about.'

OK then.

Kate and I are organizing a big *Tatler* party. It is going to be an Art Ball, put on in partnership with Christie's auction house and filmed by the BBC. We want the party to be as decadent and wild as possible. 'It needs to have tables loaded with so much food it is almost disgusting,' I say in one of the many, many meetings we have about the party. 'Roman, orgiastic, half roast chickens that people pick up with their fingers and eat in one go, chins shiny with animal fat.'

Kate thinks this is an excellent idea. The tables will heave with roasted meats, as well as caviar, oysters, cold vodka and colder champagne.

Because it is an Art Ball we must all come dressed as a work of art. I consider something complicated, like a recreation of a Renaissance miniature of Elizabeth I, complete with circular frame; but then I think: Fuck it, turn a party dress inside out and wear that. 'Woman' by Rachel Whiteread. Empty space where a person should be. Mike wears a Leonardo da Vinci T-shirt.

It is one of those parties where your glass is never empty for long (and I drink faster than anyone I have ever met, except my father, who could down a glass of red wine and pour another one straight away, like iced water on a hot day). After innumerable glasses of champagne, I move on to vodka and tonics, doubles please. At midnight I persuade the travel editor, the only other person on the editorial team with children, to down two espresso Martinis in succession with me.

When we get home Mike holds my hair from my face as I vomit into the loo.

We go to another party. I get drunk again, this time by having a shot of sambuca between every glass of wine. I attempt to get up on to the table to dance (something I used to do in pizza restaurants on the King's Road when I was fifteen; I am now thirty-nine) but the ceiling is too low and it doesn't really work. I feel so ill in the long cab ride home, window open, my head hanging out like one of those dogs on holiday.

'Make him stop,' I say to Mike, my words slurred.

The cab stops. We are in West Norwood. I get out, bend forward, clutch my knees, try to get myself together.

'Just leave me here,' I say, thinking I can't get back into the cab, anything would be better than getting back in the cab, falling asleep here on the pavement would be better than that.

'Yes, leave her here,' says the cab driver, nervous for the interior of his car.

'Don't be crazy, get back in,' says Mike.

Another party. First we are taken out for dinner by some friends who like expensive wine. I am on some crazy diet so am not eating carbs (not even peas or carrots) but I am drinking the wine. Then we go to the party. There is a starry crowd, actors and film directors. Edward St Aubyn, the writer and famous former junkie, is there. My friend, the hostess, thinks we'll have a bit in common. 'Gav's dad was very wild, a wonderful hairdresser, and a heroin dealer in Chelsea!' she says, leaving us sitting opposite each other in a corner. I blabber a bit about Dad, the dealing, Jamie Blandford. Edward tells me a story about a drug deal involving a classic car and a corpse. We stare at each other. I find him intimidating and drink some more. I am relieved when we make our excuses and move on to people that we can talk to and it not have to be about junkies and dead people. Later that evening, after I have taken MDMA and drunk so much Laurent Perrier champagne that I will never be able to bear the taste of it again, I spot him. He is standing against a wall, observing the mayhem, the drunken, drugged dancing and smoking. Haven't you come far, daughter of a drug dealer?

My mum is staying the night, babysitting. She is asleep in our room. Mike and I have to sleep on a mattress on the floor in the girls' bedroom. I pass out and wake up an hour later. I run to the loo to vomit. Vomit again. I get a mixing bowl (the one I use to make birthday cakes for the girls) and keep it by me. I spend all night being sick into the bowl. By morning there is nothing left in my stomach and yet I am still retching, grunting noisily each time. The girls giggle and copy me.

'Who am I? Bleurgh, Bleurgh?'

'Mummy!'

14

1990, London

I met him on one of those wild nights when Anya told her mother she was staying at mine and I told my mother that I was staying at Anya's (they never called each other to check, our mothers). This scheme offered great freedom; it meant we could stay out all night and do whatever we wanted with whomever we wanted. But there was also jeopardy. No one knew where we were and we couldn't go home when we'd had enough. Often we would end up at the twenty-four-hour cinema in King's Cross, laid out on the floor, trying to sleep on crushed popcorn and spilled beer, half an eye open for the film (usually one of the *Mad Max*es) and possible molesters.

We were fifteen years old, one month between our birthdays, but we looked older: old enough to be sold cigarettes in the newsagents around the corner, old enough to be served Bacardi Cokes in bars, old enough to be admitted to nightclubs, often without paying, for there never were enough teenage girls in those places and they always wanted more.

When I was little I found my mother's sugar-coated contraceptives and ate them, one by one, crunching the cute pink pills between my baby teeth. I had swallowed them all by the time my parents discovered me and took me to hospital. The doctors decided not to pump my stomach. The pills wouldn't do too much harm, although I might start adolescence a little earlier than my friends, the doctors said. They were right. I was wearing a bra and got my period when I was still at primary school.

Anya and I were in a bar with green neon signage just off Leicester Square, a place full of Europeans and musicians, a party crowd. There was a small group who were having the kind of fun that we wanted, laughing and dancing. We began to talk, shouting over the music, making ourselves part of their gang. Among them was Adrian, the boy I liked, mostly because I sensed that he might like me. Drinks were put in our hands; we didn't ask what they were, we just drank, a sour taste that I recognized again when I kissed him, at the bar, the people around us whooping encouragement.

The streets were a carnival that night and we were part of it, walking down the middle of the road, bottles and cigarettes in our hands, an uproar of fun, collecting people as we went, to another bar, another club. No one asked our age, where we were from, why we were still out at 4 a.m. Soho loves a wayward young vagabond.

We stayed the night (what was left of it) in a squat on the Latimer Road estate in West Kensington. At dawn I kissed Adrian goodbye with tongues. We arranged to meet in the same bar another night soon.

At school I told people I had met a boy. After school I went to my father's basement hairdressing salon in

Knightsbridge, with its pot plants and leather armchairs. I had taken to doing this rather than going home, where grief still hung in the air like a damp fog; where at night I had panic attacks, the numbness spreading up my arms, my chest tightening so I thought I would die, the only thing for it a trip to the Chelsea and Westminster hospital A & E (again) and the calming neon lights that meant I was safe. At Dad's I could drink beer while I did my homework. Then we might go to the pub, Dad and I; anything to put off going home. I would sit with Dad and say, 'Will I ever get a boyfriend? Everyone else has a boyfriend, no one likes me, they always like the other girls.' Sometimes I would cry. He would hug me and say, 'It will happen.' Or laugh and say, 'Boys aren't that great anyway.' Sometimes my friends would come to the salon with me after school. When the clients and the other hair stylists had gone we would smoke Dad's joints and take his speed, drink his wine while he dispensed his intoxicating wisdom. 'Always remember, girls, you hold the keys to the kingdom, don't let down the drawbridge for any old Tom, Dick or Harry.'

He was talking about sex, about our virginities. And we nodded as though we were listening to him, when really our virginities were the thing we were all most desperate to lose, we didn't really care who with. At least I didn't.

'I've got a boyfriend,' I said.

Dad and I were in the salon, sitting across from each other at the reception desk, scratched mahogany with a green leather topper tooled with gold. We were working. I was making little packets for the cocaine that he sold to his friends and clients. They would come to his salon to get their hair cut or have a blow dry for a party, and collect their drugs as they left, a kiss on the cheek and a discreet palm-to-palm exchange. I was slicing the pages of fashion magazines into squares with a razor, folding the squares into neat envelopes. I was being artistic with the packages, trying to make them visually exciting so that, when folded, there would be something cool and iconographic on the front, like a pair of glossy red lips, a shoe, a conical Madonna breast. Dad would then fill the envelope with a measured gramme of cocaine mixed with crushed Pro Plus tablets. It was nearly time for my school fees to be paid and Dad needed a bit of extra cash.

'Finally! When can I meet him?'

'I don't know. Soon, I suppose.'

'If he hurts you I'll break his kneecaps.'

'For God's sake, Dad!'

'Do you want another line?'

'Go on then.'

I met Adrian's parents before he met mine.

Adrian lived on the Tulse Hill estate, in a barely furnished flat, the decrepitude of which – torn wallpaper, moulding sofa, peeling floor tiles, stained bathtub – was unmitigated by any personal touches like a cheap ethnic throw or Bob Marley poster. The flat had been given to him by the council when he had left care six months earlier. He wanted to work in the film industry, carried a second-hand copy of Verlaine in the pocket of his too-long greatcoat and listened to Chopin on his stereo. There was a single bed in his room that I sometimes shared. We did not have sex. Instead I would go through his things when he went out, searching for a different route to intimacy. At the back of a drawer I found documentation from his time in care; I learnt that his parents were unstable alcoholics. I read the notes from the child psychologist that talked about how Adrian preferred to create fantasy worlds with his Star Wars toys than live in the real one. I understood that. I spent years playing Dungeons and Dragons, giving myself a new name, a new identity: invincible warrior queen.

One night his mother came over when I was there. I tried to be charming, to play the game of meeting my boyfriend's parents. Adrian's mother had blonde hair greased into a thin ponytail, and a swollen face red with booze and rage. It was impossible to tell how old she was, in her late sixties or in her early thirties. Her stomach was bloated but her legs were emaciated. She didn't even see me, I don't think, her eyes roving and incapable of focus. She was drunk and staggering. She shouted at her son, swore at him, then they collapsed into each other crying; she stroked his hair and he laid his head in her lap, whimpering. Adrian always said to me that we humans only tell the truth about ourselves when we are smashed. I felt I shouldn't be there, I definitely shouldn't be watching, but I couldn't keep my eyes off them. Finally I had found somewhere worse than my own house. Finally I had found someone more damaged than me.

I think that was what I saw in him.

I told my friends at school that Adrian was now my boyfriend, even though sometimes we would arrange to meet and he wouldn't turn up. Sometimes when we were together he would talk to other girls and I could see something in his eyes that I never saw when he looked at me. That pain felt familiar too.

There was a party. An older guy called Rosco who had been hanging around with Dad was selling his flat in Pont Street, or he was renting and was moving out, it wasn't clear, but the flat would be empty except for the imitation Matisse paintings on the walls and the bar and we were all invited, me, my dad and 'all your pretty little friends'. I invited Adrian and his crowd too. I wanted to show him a bit of my life. I thought maybe the shiny decadence of it would make me more attractive, or at least give us something to laugh about, all the silly old men with their fat wallets chasing young girls.

Dad and I were having dinner first. It was a Friday night. Dad had some friends over from the old days in Spain, when he ran a hairdressing salon in Marbella. They were tanned and rich-looking in a retro criminal kind of way, cream suits and gold signet rings, muscular hands that looked as though they could strangle a man (or a woman). The wine they bought in the pub was more expensive than the stuff we usually got. Dad was pleased to see them. There was talk about people they'd known. Dad's accent changed when he spoke to them: it became more like theirs. I didn't speak much, I just watched, holding the beer bottle to my lips. There was a woman with them who didn't speak much either. She was the girlfriend of one of the gangsters, short and petite but with huge breasts that made her look unstable, as if she might topple forward when she stood. She wore a ruched Lycra miniskirt and old-fashioned stockings with a black line up the back for an intrepid index finger to follow. Her patent stilettos were so hard to walk in that the traffic had to stop for her as she tiptoed across the road from the pub to San Lorenzo, where the gangsters were joining us for dinner. We went through the black-tiled entrance into the restaurant, which was like entering a parallel world, because suddenly we were in the Mediterranean. There were lilies and palms, a fan whirring gently above. We sat at a round table in the upper balcony with white linen and heavy silver crockery.

'This was where me and Jan had our wedding reception,' Dad explained.

'I remember,' said one of the gangsters. 'How is she?'

'She got fat,' said Dad.

'Shame.'

It was exciting to be there, to drink the white wine that was so cold the glass sweated, to eat the creamy asparagus risotto, to listen to the stories, the ones they told about the semi-famous people they knew out in Spain, the rockers and bank robbers, the pools and affairs. Eventually, Dad turned his attention towards Ali, the girl. She was heavily made up with sparkly powders, pinks and blues. Her ash-blonde hair was piled upon her head in airy, lacquered whorls.

'So, what do you do, my darling?'

She looked at him in surprise, and then smiled, a delicious side smile that showed off unexpectedly small, pearly teeth.

'Don't take the piss,' said one of the gangsters.

Dad stared at her. She lowered her eyes, so heavy with mascara I thought she might not be able to lift them again. She looked at her tits.

'Fuck, sorry, darling, of course.'

She was, it transpired, a famous page-three model.

'Jan did a bit of page three, in the early days, along with Viv and Jilly.'

'Trailblazers,' she said sweetly, and smiled at me, as if this information had made me part of her world. I smiled back, pleased by the air of sophistication this new connection gave me. Perhaps Ali would come to the party and I could introduce her to Adrian. What would he make of that!

'It's a real pleasure to meet you in the flesh . . .' said Dad and he took one of Ali's pale, tiny hands with the sharp red nails, gently pulled it to his mouth and kissed it, holding her hand to his lips much longer than was necessary. He let go and took a gulp of wine. 'So, can I see them?' he said.

Ali giggled. I watched her meet eyes with her scary boyfriend, his little nod.

She then gracefully unclipped two hidden fastenings at the front of her dress. She was not wearing a bra but her breasts did not droop at all on being released from their confinement – they remained almost impossibly buoyant, two vast milky orbs with very pale pink nipples. I felt my own chest constrict. This was happening, at dinner; people could see. And yet Ali didn't rush to close her top, she let my father's gaze linger on her body, as well as that of everyone else nearby. Waiters serving adjacent tables laid down plates of food with their heads turned. I remembered a thing a teacher had told me, about when the Greeks were going home after the Trojan War. Menelaus had his recaptured wife Helen on his boat and went at her with a dagger, intending to kill her for all the death and destruction her beauty has caused. But Helen simply pulled apart her gown, showed Menelaus her perfect tits, and he stayed his hand; he fucked her instead of killing her.

'Beautiful,' said Dad, raising a glass. 'Thank you.'

'Pleasure,' Ali replied, and refastened her dress with an easy movement that suggested she had done this a million times before.

Dinner was going on longer than expected, with coffees and cognacs which came in massive bowl-like glasses, the golden liquid coating the inside of the glasses as the gangsters swirled them in their tanned hands, interspersing gulps of liquor with sucks on their cigars. Dad had a cigar too. He offered me a puff, which I took even though I hated the smell and it made me nauseous. He passed me a packet of cocaine under the table and I went to the white marble loos to do a line, aware of the serious and rich-looking older women waiting outside. The coke made me jittery, worried that Adrian was already at Rosco's house, flirting with my friends.

The gangsters had got the bill by the time I was back at

the table. Dad was thanking them for dinner, not getting out his cheque book. We left in a hurry to be sure of avoiding paying our share. At the exit I waited for Dad to walk down the steps first; the paparazzi who were always waiting outside for Princess Diana or Elizabeth Hurley, or some other celebrity, lowered their big black cameras when they saw that it was only us. I wanted Dad to go down the steps first because I had got it into my head that I might slip and the back of my skull would crack against the hard granite step-edge and I might die, right there in Beauchamp Place, while the paparazzi watched and didn't know if this was something they should take a photograph of and my dad cradled me as he had my sister.

I was always imagining things like this, the worst thing that could possibly happen.

I managed the steps without incident.

Adrian was not at the party yet, but Anya and Bella were there, sitting on the floor because there were no chairs, drinking from a bottle of wine because there were no glasses, flicking their ash on to the white carpet because there were no ashtrays. They were with another girl, Kitty, who was at school with Bella, pretty and dark with an absurdly slender waist, of the sort that men like to encircle with their hands, of the sort that turns a girl into a possession. Kitty was explaining how she had kissed Prince, Gary Stretch and Billy Idol (not all at once, on separate occasions). I was impressed and a little envious. Maybe this was just what happened if you had a waist like that.

We had run out of wine so I went to the bar to get another bottle. Dad was at the bar with his friend

Alethea, and she was whispering in his ear while watching the people in the room nervously. She smiled when she saw me though, and gave me a hug. Her father was Lord Chief Justice or something, which always made Dad laugh. He and Alethea left the main room, looking for somewhere more private to continue their conversation. I went behind the bar and took a bottle of wine from an ice bucket.

The party was busier now, a strange mixture of fusty middle-aged Sloanes, sleek Euros and dodgy-looking types who worked in the local shops and pubs. I kept looking around, hoping to see Adrian, and it was as though he appeared from nowhere, because suddenly he was there, a dark presence looming in the doorway. I fetched him and brought him to sit down with our group, offered him the bottle of wine, which he held to his lips for a long time, not seeming to care that he was finishing it and we were meant to be sharing. He smelt of three-day-old rum and cigarettes. He seemed angry, as if he was here under duress. But his mood softened when he saw Kitty, Bella and Anya: their long hair, their made-up eyes, their lovely young bodies.

It upset me, sitting there, watching him watching them, so I went to get more wine. On the way I decided to look for Dad. I wanted to introduce him to Adrian. But I got a bit lost, going into different rooms where he never was, finding people talking who looked up at me as if I was intruding, or people embracing who didn't stop kissing and groping even though I stared. I was surprised by how big the place was, all the corridors and doors, and I was more drunk than was enjoyable, lurching and bumping along walls. For a time I panicked because I couldn't work out how to locate the main party room again, but I made myself breathe and focus, followed the sounds of music and voices, and found my way back there. The crowds had thinned out a little now. Adrian was still sitting on the floor, looking like a pile of rags, but, instead of the girls, I saw that Dad was with him. I smiled. Dad must have seen the girls, gone to sit down, been introduced, and now he was chatting with Adrian. The two men in my life. And then I saw the look on Adrian's face. I went closer and realized that he was shouting at Dad, talking about me, twisting some of the things I had told him about us, telling Dad he was a bad man, a bad father, that he should look after me better, it was his responsibility. Dad caught my eye. He pulled himself up off the ground.

'I'm still talking to you,' said Adrian.

'And I'm bored of listening to you,' he replied.

When Dad walked past me he was holding himself differently; he seemed to have grown denser, stockier, his muscles bunched up in preparation for a fight.

'Your boyfriend wants to beat me up,' he said.

'Oh,' I said, sorry, embarrassed, confused, unable to work out which extreme emotion should take prominence in my heart.

I would have gone with Adrian that night. But he said no, he had other places to be, other people to meet. So Dad and I took a cab home and I felt drunk and exhausted, my head bouncing against the hard black interior of the taxi, Dad staring out into the night, still tense and angry, like someone I didn't know.

In the week that followed I tried calling Adrian but his Marxist flatmate always answered and said he wasn't there. Eventually Adrian himself answered, sounding surprised that it was me, as if he didn't know that I had been calling every day, sometimes twice.

'I'm in trouble. It looks like I might end up in prison,' he said.

'Oh God, that's awful. Let me help.'

'There's nothing you can do.'

'Yes there is. I can talk to my dad – he knows people.'

'That won't help.'

'How long do you think you'll have to go to prison for?'

'About a year. I'll call when I get out.'

'When will you go into prison? Can I see you before you go?'

'No.'

A couple of months later Anya and I were going up the escalator at Brixton Tube station. It was about 11 p.m. Once again I had told my mother I was staying at Anya's and she had told her mother she was staying at mine. We were going to the Fridge nightclub. Anya had been flirting with the DJ who worked there and he had put us on the guest list. We liked dancing to the new song, 'Gypsy Woman' by Crystal Waters. We didn't know where we would go after the club; we would see where the night took us.

As I was going up I saw Adrian going down the

escalator on the other side. He was with a woman. She was beautiful, wearing baggy jeans, slipping her hand into her pocket and passing something to him in a way that was so intimate that I knew they were together.

He'd pretended that he was going to prison, that was how much he didn't want to be with me. That was how absurd and fucked up he was. That was how unappealing I was. But that night I didn't care, that night I could laugh about it, because I drank alcohol, took drugs, danced, and didn't go home.

15

2015, London

It is 5.30 a.m. My husband and children are asleep in their beds. I am in the sitting room, my laptop on my knees, a cup of green tea balanced on the armrest. I am still in my pyjamas, although I am wearing the jumper and woollen socks that I laid out for myself last night and found in the dark this morning.

I am awake because I have made a decision to devote myself more zealously to writing the story of my childhood. I have been doing this for months but still nothing makes any sense. I can't pull the disparate threads into a satisfying narrative order; they are just getting more tangled and confused. I still haven't found Candy and I still haven't found any sort of peace. Quite the opposite. I feel jangly and detached, only just keeping a lid on the spewing mayhem in my head, holding on to my husband and children so hard, as though they are some sort of lifeline to reality.

The solution must be to try harder. This is the only thing that has ever worked for me. Keep grafting, never give up, believe in yourself, you'll get there in the end, you always do.

My plan is to wake up at 5 a.m. at least three days a

week to write, as well as writing on the way to work and at weekends. I will be doing this in addition to editing a magazine. Kate has gone on maternity leave and I am now the editor of *Tatler*. I have a staff of thirty, my own office and a young girl whose main job, it seems, is to make me cups of tea.

Dad would be so proud. He would tell everyone I was running the whole of Condé Nast.

I have been trying to organize things chronologically, as this seems the best and simplest way, rather than being jazzy and trying to do it alphabetically or themat-ically (drugs, death, sex . . .), but on this morning I find I have come to an impasse. And that impasse is my other sister.

The night Dad met Mum, he wasn't just driving back to London from Marbella, he was leaving behind his family: his common-law wife and baby girl.

Gavin met Kerstin on the beach in the early seven-ties. Back then southern Spain was a retreat for all sorts of hippies and freaks, bare-footed bohemians in the sun, barely aware that Franco was still in charge. Kerstin was a nineteen-year-old Swedish model, a skinny blue-eyed blonde in cut-off denim shorts who loved getting high, didn't really matter how. Dad was already burnt out at twenty-five. He had been a hairdressing star when he was working at the London salons, Evansky's and Leon-ard's, famous for his immaculate up-dos and ebullient chair-side manner, a slim-hipped fixture on the sixties scene, partying at nightclubs like Sybilla's and the Are-thusa, friends with actors and musicians (he always claimed he was the inspiration for the philandering hair-dresser character played by Warren Beatty in the 1975 film, *Shampoo*). But he had fallen in love with a sixteen-year-old debutante and show jumper called Jayne Harries. They had eloped to Gibraltar to marry, chased by the paparazzi, and had laid low in Marrakech with the Rolling Stone Brian Jones. Not long after they returned to London, to race through her inheritance on fast cars and hard drugs. The relationship soon imploded (Harries would later die of a drugs overdose in a public loo in Cranleigh aged twenty-four). Dad had come to Spain to mend his heart and make the most of the hash and heroin that came direct from Morocco. He opened a hairdressing salon called Gotama (he had never read Hermann Hesse, he just knew the name was kind of groovy). Kerstin couldn't speak much English and he couldn't speak any Swedish, but they fell for each other anyway. They made love, took drugs, hung out. One day Kerstin strolled out on to the motorway into the path of an oncoming car. Dad rushed to push her out of the way and was run over himself. When he tried to stand he realized that his foot was pointing in the wrong direc-tion. Kerstin went back to Sweden. Gavin convalesced, his leg in plaster, his waistline expanding, his girl far away. She wrote him letters complaining about a stom-ach ache that turned out to be a pregnancy; he wrote her a letter begging her to keep their baby.

Kerstin was an addict during her pregnancy and their baby Maranda was born an addict too. According to the stories, the surgeons inserted a tube into her stomach and via this tube they were able to flush away the opiated maternal blood that ran in her tiny veins and replace it with clean blood, so that baby Maranda wouldn't have to endure the dangerous agony of cold turkey. The family were reunited in Spain, but in less than a year they separated. Dad came back to London and Kerstin returned to Stockholm with their baby. On his way back he met Mum and soon conceived me, replacing one lost daughter with a new one.

When I was little I knew I had a sister in Sweden but I rarely saw her. Sometimes when Kerstin was going through a rough patch with booze and drugs Maranda would come and stay with us (I was too young to remember these trips). When I was nine I went to visit her in Stockholm. All I can remember is eating the delicious cream and potato pie that Maranda's grandmother cooked, and hoovering a spotless flat to Abba turned up loud on the stereo.

Dad was a bad father to Maranda, only starting to pay maintenance when he was ordered to by the court (she was fifteen and he had to back-pay three thousand pounds). Kerstin was unstable, alcoholic, unpredictable. One afternoon, when Maranda was sixteen, she asked her mother for some help with her homework.

'I'll help you when I get back. I am just going out to buy some food,' she replied.

She didn't return.

Maranda remained in the flat in Stockholm for a couple of weeks, waiting for her mother. Then she went to live with her grandmother. One day she decided she wanted to come to England. She had another family there, didn't she, one that might be less fucked up than her family in Sweden.

Maranda came to live with us in Battersea less than a year after Candy died. She couldn't have found a more fucked-up family if she'd tried.

She was put in Candy's room and told not to move Candy's things. She wanted to learn how to be a hairdresser, to be like her dad, so he gave her a job at his salon in Knightsbridge. She washed hair, swept hair, made endless cups of tea for clients. She saw her father selling drugs, she saw him taking drugs, she saw him giving drugs to his other daughter and flirting with his daughter's friends. She suspected that he was doing more than flirting.

She tried to clean the flat where they lived; she found the dirt and the squalor disgusting. At weekends she would scrub the bath, but it never seemed to get properly clean. She tried to make friends with her sister, but found her uncommunicative, angry, drunk, high, or just not there.

She felt sad and lonely. Her stepmother would buy her sister new clothes, but there was never anything for her.

There are conflicting reports of what happened next. Maranda was a challenging teenager who'd had a difficult childhood. She was desperate for love, but found none. My mother couldn't handle her and our father didn't want to. He was busy with other, less confrontational, young women. Maranda was thrown out of the flat, leaving late at night in the rain, her possessions in two black plastic bags. 'You have tried to destroy this family,' Dad said, even though he was the one who was destroying the family, what was left of it.

Maranda found a place to stay, a squat in Camden. She started work at a different hairdressing salon, continuing her training. When she went back to see my father, to ask him for a bit of money, he gave her amphetamines to sell.

I find this hard to write not just because it is hard, but also because I cannot remember any of it.

I know that Maranda lived in our flat, in Candy's room, but I have no recollection of this. I cannot remember standing in the kitchen with her in the mornings eating Marmite on toast, or sitting on the sofa with her in the evenings watching *Minder*. Maranda worked in Dad's salon in Knightsbridge, a place where I spent a great deal of time, but I cannot remember seeing her there.

I don't know why memory and sisters are so weird and slippery for me. The only thing I can remember about me and Maranda as teenagers was a holiday in Ibiza. Maranda had got into an empty bath and cried because I refused to go clubbing with her.

'I just want to go dancing with my sister,' wailed Maranda.

'No,' I said.

'Dance with me,' said Candy, her brown eyes hopeful.

'No,' I said.

I don't know what my relationship with Candy would have been like. I cannot imagine the shape of that loss. So much would have been different had she not died that the absence of a close relationship with a woman who shares my past has never seemed like the most fundamental part of my story. But perhaps it is. And the fact is I do have a sister, one who is alive.

Maranda is now a successful hairdresser living in Los Angeles. We barely communicate. I see her about once every two years when she visits London for work. We usually get drunk.

I decide not to include her in the stories I am writing. They are complicated enough already.

16

1990, London

It was a Sunday in summer and we were going for a family lunch at our favourite restaurant, Leonardo's. The night before Anya and I had gone to a party in a garden square in Notting Hill and had somehow ended up in a house that looked like a museum in Holland Park, sitting around a table drinking Thunderbird with people we had never met before. I drank so much that when I stood up I realized that I couldn't walk and I had to crawl out on my hands and knees to leave, laughing as I went.

'Hello! Everybody, hello!' said the restaurant owner, Paco, taking our coats from us as we entered the restaurant. He had black eyebrows and white hair and was so tall that when I was little I made a game of running between his legs.

'Hello, my darling,' said Dad.

Paco turned to Mum. He held her by her shoulders and kissed her on each cheek; then he touched my hair as though I was still a little girl.

He made a small 'follow me' gesture with his hand.

Our table was by the window. The restaurant smelt of fried garlic, bread sticks, cigarette smoke and red wine spilt on thick cotton tablecloths. The smells were as familiar to me as the sounds, the clink of cutlery, the noise of corks being popped, the trundle of the metallic dessert trolley, constantly wheeled about with its wobbly trifles, *torta della nonna* and profiteroles.

We had been coming here since I was a baby, every weekend. We came for celebrations, for birthdays, for New Year's Eve. There were always friends at the other tables, and they would stop by our table for a chat, pull up a chair to sit with us and have a glass of wine: Sarah, Michael, Quentin, Andy (although he was dead now too, tipped his chair and smashed his head on the stone dining-room floor at John Jermyn's Tuscan villa, was put to bed, no one checked on him, cold by morning). We came here with our family, my grandparents unsure of the exotic menu, my grandmother asking if she could just have a prawn cocktail. The waiters – Paco, Pepe, the tall one with the glasses who had attended Candy's cremation – they all called me *bambina*, even though I was fifteen years old and hungover with black eye make-up on my cheeks, even though they were Spanish and not Italian.

Our table had been laid for four people and Paco whipped away the unnecessary crockery, handing it all to a passing waiter as though it was radioactive.

'I think we should eat what she would have eaten,' said Mum. 'Artichokes to start and then spaghetti vongole.'

'Why?' I asked, looking at them both. Dad was staring out of the window, his lips tense. Mum raised her eyes to meet mine.

'Today is your sister's birthday.'

Candy always ate artichokes and spaghetti vongole at Leonardo's.

Paco was standing behind Dad, his hands on the back of his chair, looking mournful in an over-the-top Mediterranean way. He knew the right thing to do; he knew how to grieve. They teach them that in Spain.

'Artichoke to start and then spaghetti vongole, for three,' said Mum.

Paco nodded solemnly, as if to say: Yes, this will be the most delicious and the most tragic food you will ever eat.

I didn't want artichoke and spaghetti vongole. I couldn't think of anything I wanted less. I didn't even want Italian food. Why did we have to keep coming here? Why did she keep doing this to us?

'Do you think Candy would mind if we had some wine?' I asked.

Mum tutted. Dad winked at me.

'Can we have a bottle of Gavi di Gavi,' I said to the next waiter who passed.

The artichokes were delivered to our table. A spiky flower in a bath of warm butter. We did not speak as we pulled at the thick petals, scraped at the lip of flesh with our teeth, butter dripping down our chins in a way that was undignified and inappropriate. The morsels got stuck in my throat; the sharp-crusted bread that I dunked in the melted butter made my eyes water. The smaller, flimsier petals in the middle needed to be pulled out in clumps, the hairy choke discarded, although it still stuck to my fingers.

Mum started to cry as she ate, fat, rolling tears that

plopped into the coagulating butter. I stared down at the table and made a sort of 'mmmm' sound because I was embarrassed and I didn't know what to do or what to say and I did wish that she would stop crying before the other people in the restaurant noticed what was happening and were put off their food too.

Dad pushed his plate away. 'Candy wouldn't have wanted this,' he said. 'She was never down in the dumps, was she?' He picked up the wine bottle and refilled my glass and his, right to the rim. He held up the empty bottle and waved it. When Paco wound his way through the restaurant to our table Dad told him that he wanted something different: calves' liver and spinach and sautéed potatoes, and another bottle of wine. So I changed my order as well.

'Can I have chicken Kiev, and some spinach too?'

'Of course, no problem, that is no problem at all.'

Sad people are allowed to change their minds. Sad people can do any fucking thing they like and no one is allowed to complain because they don't know how it feels.

I cut into the chicken Kiev and the garlic butter squirted up like lava from a volcano, trickling down the bread-crusted exterior, still bubbly and hot. I drank more wine, shovelled food into my mouth, began to feel good again, the sort of reckless, crazed joy that you feel when you know you are not allowed to be happy but you suddenly discover that you are. Contraband happiness. I laughed with my mouth open, smoked cigarettes, stumbled downstairs to the loo, checked out the handsome guys at the bar as I made my way back to our table.

Dad and I ate zabaglione, spooning the sweet, alcoholic froth into our mouths, sucking it up through the biscuit that was like a straw that came with it. We ordered flaming sambucas, the fire blue, curling and shimmering on the top of the liquid, the alcohol sizzling on the edge of the glass. I crunched the warm coffee beans with my teeth, drank the sweet, thick, aniseedy drink, ordered another. I felt so drunk that it seemed as if I was sinking into the wickerwork seat of my chair. We smoked more cigarettes, lit the amaretti biscuit wrappers so they floated up like Chinese lanterns, smudging the ceiling with grey ash, making the few remaining diners lean back in their chairs, watch and smile at the most fun people in the restaurant, me and my dad. And all the while Mum sat there, looking at nothing, not smiling, even at our most outrageous displays of fun, eating the strawberry ice-cream so slowly, mouthful by awful mouthful, broken glass on her tongue, sharp bits of metal going down her throat.

'Can we just go now,' she said finally, her voice cracking. She covered her eyes with her hands and her shoulders began to move up and down.

17

2015, London

I am taking a meeting about a new supplement that *Tatler*'s advertising department would like us to produce. I have been acting editor of the magazine for nearly six months.

There are about fifteen people in the meeting.

'So, let's begin,' I say.

I lick my lips and taste blood. I put my hand over my mouth.

I've had psoriasis for years, itchy red skin that becomes more inflamed when I am stressed and under pressure. Until now it has only ever been behind my ears and about the nape of my neck. Hidden, like all my other murky secrets. But lately it has spread to my lips. They have become dry and swollen. I treat them with a mild steroid cream, but sometimes they crack and bleed and everyone can see.

I am still getting up at 5 a.m. most mornings to write, after nights when anxiety about work has kept me awake. Some days the writing calms me, a controlled trance, the words coming like slow honey, and it all makes sense, I can do it. Some days the words are jagged and I want to stop but then one of the girls stumbles into the sitting room, up early, looking for me, and I tuck them under a blanket and tell them to sleep for a bit longer, Mummy is working. They smile and close their eyes. I think they like the tap tap tap sound of me at my computer. Other days I am so mad and pent up, I feel as if I am standing on the edge of a cliff even though I am in a white office with a white desk and big windows overlooking Hanover Square.

I am more and more afraid. When the phone rings I am sure it is news that someone I love has died. The school call: I assume that Hebe has had a horrible accident. Mike is fifteen minutes late coming home from work: I am convinced he has had a bike accident and is dead. I call and call and when he doesn't answer I accept my new reality with cool composure, working out what I will do, how I will tell the children, how I will pay the mortgage by myself (wishing I had listened when Mike said we should get life insurance, you should get a pension, why am I always so resistant to conformity, the idea that people might get old in a normal way?). I sense that I am detaching myself from him and the life that we have created together. I do this again and again, every time he is late, putting my love for him in a box and closing it up because it is too painful to keep inside me. I have done this before, I tell myself, I have survived grave loss and I can do it again, but only if I stop this crazy indulgence of loving people who die.

When he walks through the door, holding his bike helmet, I go slack with relief. I do not tell him quite how far my worries have taken me, but he is learning that whenever he calls the first thing he must say is 'everything is OK'. And I believe him, I really do. For now.

I try to control these feelings, I try to not let them show, especially around my children. They are clever little animals and they can sense that I am closing myself off. I try to be fun and brave and silly for them. Fake it to make it. I take Hebe to Florence for a weekend and we eat pizzas and ice-cream, go to an old-fashioned stationer's to watch them hand-marble paper, spend an afternoon in the Uffizi taking photographs of all the naked bottoms. We have so much fun.

I don't want them to see that I am cracking. I want them to believe that I am solid. Even though it is not true.

'Excuse me,' I say, dabbing the blood away with a tissue and applying the moisturizing lip balm that I now keep on me at all times. Then I force myself to smile.

18

1991, London

Our school bags were piled in the corner, spilling over with lever-arch files and scrawled-on textbooks. There was black kohl weeping around our eyes and our pin-striped shirts were unbuttoned down to our black M&S bras. We did not wear tights or socks, just bare legs, shaved, with smudgy fake tan and scuffed black loafers.

It was too hot. There were three fans going in the salon at once, blowing the hot air around, making tiny whirlpools of the cut hair on the tiled floor.

'It's the Nymphets!' Dad said as he stomped down the narrow stairs. He was holding two bottles of wine and had two fresh packets of cigarettes, one in either back pocket. There was a sheen on his forehead and damp patches in the hair around his temples. It was eight o'clock in the evening, still light outside, but we were all down here, in Dad's hairdressing salon. The clients and the other hairdressers had gone and the basement was ours. We put on rave music and used the edges of our school shirts to wipe the beads of moisture from our upper lips.

'Gav!' said Polly. She was the sister of one of my friends. She stood up and wrapped her hands around the two bottles of wine and kissed Dad on either cheek, proper lip-to-skin kisses. I thought about how sweaty his skin would be. They stood for a moment. So close. There was so much that I chose to ignore.

'This is Julia,' she said, finally moving away from him, taking the bottles and putting them on the reception desk.

'Hi,' said Julia, scooping an armful of her blonde hair and flicking it from one side of her head to the other.

My father reached for her hand and brought it to his mouth. He kissed her knuckles.

'Welcome to the madhouse,' he said.

Dad manoeuvred around the teenage limbs, making his way to his chair behind the desk. He turned up the music, closed the appointment book and put it in the drawer. He cleared the debris, bits of hair and loose tobacco, off the green leather with a cupped hand. He lifted out of his chair a little and reached into his back pocket, getting his wallet.

'So, ladies, who wants a line?'

'Me!' 'Me!' 'Me!' 'Me!'

'Me,' I said.

I slid my eyes sideways and saw Julia laughing with disbelief as my father took the fat, tightly folded packet of cocaine from his wallet. He opened it and shook half the contents on to the desk, dividing the white powder using his Gold American Express Card, making six messy lines. He rolled a pink fifty-pound note into a straw and snorted the biggest line, rubbing his nose afterwards so the cartilage squeaked. He passed the rolled-up note to me. As his daughter I did still have some privileges. I stood, deciding which line to go for. I didn't want the largest one; I wanted the one with the fewest lumps. I was paranoid about rocks of coke getting lodged in my nasal canal, even though I snorted water every night before going to bed, just like Daddy taught me.

I bent forwards and did a line, I felt the chemical taste hit the back of my palate and my throat go numb. I liked the intensity of it, the pop in my brain. I gulped red wine to get rid of the taste and watched as everyone else took their turn, bending forwards over the table, each of them, one by one, in front of my father, their shirts falling open, while he watched and twinkled with deep satisfaction.

Afterwards we talked nonsense, shouting over each other, no one listening to anything anyone else was saying. When we started chewing our words, when drunkenness began to overwhelm the coke high, Dad got out more drugs. Sarah went up to the pub for more wine. Julia told us about a boy we all sort of knew who'd been caught dealing speed and was going to be expelled, maybe even prison.

'Poor lad,' said Dad. 'But he won't get long. He's young enough.'

Anya was washing Cathy's hair because she had got too hot and wanted to cool down. Two older guys had come down, Sal and Chris, who worked at the dry cleaner's, and they were talking to Polly and Julia, their heads close together so they could hear each other over the noise of the music. I was smoking a joint because my heart had gone mad, but I had misjudged how much hash to use and now I was too stoned and the music was entering one ear and exiting the other as if there was a pipe that went through my brain, and that didn't seem like a good thing. I kept thinking that I could hear people whispering mean things about me, a swishy sound like a breeze through palm leaves that sometimes coalesced into words like 'fat' and 'bitch'. Sometimes I thought that people only wanted to be my friend so they could come down here after school.

'Fuck, I've got to go,' said Sarah, standing, swaying from the lack of oxygen at altitude. Her lips and tongue were swollen and purple from the wine. 'I've got English tomorrow.'

'Have I got that too?' said Anya, standing up and sitting straight back down again as if she had been pushed.

'Well, I haven't got any exams, so I can stay,' said Polly.

'Me too,' said Julia.

'I haven't got any exams either!' said Chris, who was forty-five and thought he was funnier than he actually was.

Sal laughed.

'Have you got an exam tomorrow?' Dad asked me.

I had to think for a moment. My head was spinning, a wide arc that felt as if it was taking me nearly all the way around the room.

'Latin,' I said. 'First thing.' I hiccuped, giggled, put a hand over my mouth. 'Shit,' I said.

Dad passed me the rolled fifty-pound note.

'Get yourself a cab home, Chubbs. We don't want you

fucking up your exams, not after all the money we've spent on your education.'

I took the note, dusted off the cocaine, flattened it, folded it in half, found my bag and put it in my purse. I had to do everything slowly, with great focus and purpose. I didn't want people to realize quite how fucked I really was. I said goodbye in a blur of kisses and arms. I walked upstairs slowly, concentrating on taking one step, then another. I realized I needed to wee so I kept going, up to the tiny loo, which somehow contained all the smells of Dad's salon – perming solution, bleach, hairspray – even though it was two floors away. I locked the door and stared at myself in the mirror. My face looked as though it was made of wax. I felt so disconnected from the person I was looking at that I was surprised, on pushing at my cheek with my finger, to feel pressure there. I laughed at myself, at the whole evening, the whole situation, my whole life. In less than twelve hours I would be sitting my Latin GCSE, and here I was completely off my face. It was insane. It was hilarious.

I made myself sick in the bushes outside our block of flats because I didn't want to use the loo at home. I didn't want Mum to hear me and come out and check on me.

'Gavanndra, is that you, are you OK?' she called out from the darkness of her room. My parents didn't share a bedroom any more. Dad had moved into Candy's old room, stapled purple fabrics to the ceiling and decorated it to look like a harem, a den of iniquity. Mum was still in their old room, with the pale blue fitted cupboards and the pictures of Jesus, which were new.

131

'Everything's fine. Go back to sleep.'

It took all my willpower to make myself sound sober, fresh, together.

'Is your father with you?'

'He stayed out with Sal and Chris. He'll be back soon.'

I was still drunk when I got on the bus to school the next morning. Still drunk when I went to the changing rooms, where we had to gather before going into the exam, which was being held in the gym.

Girls started to congregate in groups by the door, each holding a clear plastic bag containing pens, ink, pencils, sharpener, rubber, lip balm, tissues. I just had a biro behind my ear. Inside the gym the blue crash mats were all piled in a corner, princess and the pea style. Thick ropes with rubberized ends hung from the bars of the metal frame that rose all the way up to the ceiling, ropes that I had never been able to pull myself up. I always failed in here. The hall was ordered with rows of wooden chairs and desks, each with a sheet of white paper lying face down.

I found my seat. Kate, the girl in front of me, was already sitting down, her body tense as though she was about to start a race. I placed my biro in the pen-shaped groove at the top of the desk. I felt fidgety, uncomfortable, as if a mistake had been made and I had been poured into the wrong body. The hall was noisy with the sound of chairs being dragged across the wooden floor, entrance doors swinging, girls whispering. At eight fifty-nine, when we were all seated, the room fell silent except for the sound of the clock ticking and the shouts of the younger girls on the hockey pitch outside, carried on the clear summer air.

'You may now turn over your papers.'

The feeling started in my fingers, an icy numbness that spread up my limbs so that soon I was just a torso, with no sensation in my arms or legs.

I read the passage again. What the fuck was going on? I'd assumed I knew this book of *The Aeneid* so well. The start of it at least: 'Infandum, regina . . .' 'Terrible, O queen, is the sadness that you ask me to recount . . .' Those lines, that opening section, had always made me feel as though I was actually there, reclining on a soft couch in a coastal palace in Phoenicia, a palace built by a great and beautiful queen, the sound of the sea crashing against the rocks, little oil lamps all around, the glossy Phoenicians staring at battle-scarred Aeneas and his men as if they were a different species. Food, wine, laughter, music, and then the hush, the faces turned, as he began to tell his story, of a city doomed by the gods to be destroyed by the Greeks, of skulls split open with swords and babies thrown from balconies. As Aeneas spoke, as the words fell from his mouth like nuggets of gold, Dido fell in love with him, and so did everyone.

'Excellent work, Gavanndra,' Miss Yeats had said, more than once, after I had translated my lines.

But not this time. I had no recollection of these mysterious words, random collections of letters. I looked up. Kate was already writing. I looked back down. Had I translated this section once? I must have done. But maybe

133

this was something that had come up on one of the days I had taken off sick, one of those mornings when I woke up and decided I just couldn't be bothered.

'Mum, I don't feel very well.'

'OK, darling, you stay in bed, look after yourself.'

She wasn't taking any chances with me.

I read the passage again. I started translating. I knew the words I was writing made no sense, but I had to continue. I made up sentences that sounded as if they could be translated bits of Latin, things having been done, glittering swords and grey-eyed goddesses, and I wrote them with a hand that was numb, with handwriting that was strange and spiky.

I finished before the allotted time. Kate was still writing. I felt so deeply tired, the sort of tiredness that never came to me when I needed it, when I was wide awake at 3 a.m. and my thoughts rushed and crashed. I hadn't felt tiredness like this since . . . I couldn't remember when. I laid my head on the hard desk, on top of the piece of paper, and I fell asleep, the words entering my brain so I dreamt of foreign beaches and broken cities and exhausted men who wore armour that was rusted and useless.

I was woken by the sound of chairs being pushed back, by chatter that swelled out of nowhere the moment the exam finished.

'You are such a show-off, falling asleep,' said Anya. 'I could hear you snoring; it put me right off.'

I was holding my biro, aware of a sense of doom in my stomach. I had to kill that feeling before it could unfurl and grow. I chucked my pen on the floor. I wanted the plastic to smash and shard, but it just rolled under a desk.

'You weirdo,' said Anya.

It was over. Our last exam. We flew out of the exam hall into the sunshine. We ran, like a pack, out on to the empty hockey pitch. The air was thick with pollen, the earth hard and sun-baked, studded with old hockey-boot indentations. We lay in the middle of the pitch and lit Silk Cut cigarettes. Lucy produced a bottle of vodka that she had stolen from her dad's drinks cabinet. It was warm and tasted medicinal but we drank it anyway. We had taken marker pens from our form room, green, red, blue and black, and we wrote on each others' school shirts: swear words, shit, fuck, bitch; we drew pictures of tits and penises. Then we tore the shirts off each other, tore the arms off the shirts, tore them into shreds, so we were just in our bras. I felt as though I could do anything at that moment. I felt as though I could break anything that came into my hands; I wouldn't have thought twice about it. I wanted to set fire to something – all those tattered school shirts, that would be fun. Someone put a joint between my fingers and I took a drag, blew the smoke up to the blue sky. Younger girls stood on the opposite side of the fence, fingers curled around the wire, watching us. There were a couple of teachers too, but they wouldn't do anything.

And then suddenly it all became boring and uncool, and what were we doing on the hockey pitch when we could be somewhere else. The vodka had run out and we needed more cigarettes. I pulled on my jumper, the grey wool scratchy against my skin. I stuffed my torn and defaced school shirt into my bag, a memento of something. We walked out, past the few pupils who had stayed until the end, leaving fag butts and bottles and scraps of uniform for someone else to clear up. We stalked through the corridors, aggressive and restless. There was dry grass in our hair and dirt smudged on our cheeks. We bought more vodka and big bottles of Coca-Cola at the corner shop, cans of beer and cigarettes. We swaggered along hot pavements to a nearby park, dog shit and patchy grass and overflowing dustbins. We swallowed pills with the vodka and soon I was talking too quickly about things that I thought were very important and urgent, and life felt like a moment, followed by a moment, followed by a moment, all unconnected and meaningless. Someone had brought along a can of Elnett and a towel for old times' sake, and we passed this around. I inhaled the cold, tacky air from the aerosol and I kept drowning, then coming back into consciousness laughing, the canister no longer in my hands.

New people arrived: Polly and her friend Julia. They hadn't been doing exams today, their uniforms were intact, they looked smug and fresh.

'I won't actually be at Godolphin next year, we're moving to Chichester, my dad's bought this really big house,' said Julia.

'But you live with your mum,' I said, reminding everyone of Julia's ugly secret, feeling triumphant and mean as I did it.

Julia's parents were divorced, and although she talked a lot about her dad, who was a lawyer, she lived in an ex-council flat with her mother. Julia's uniform was second-hand and she didn't have a nice tennis racquet. Poverty was something to be ashamed of at our smart school. I knew that better than most.

'I'm moving in with my dad now, into a really big house,' said Julia.

'Yeah, you said,' said Anya, who was lying next to me on the grass, her head on a small, neat pillow she had made by folding her jumper.

I took a drag on a joint, the smoke molten in my lungs. I squashed the joint into the grass, burning my fingers. It was getting cold.

'So what's the plan? Shall we go down to the salon?' said Polly, looking at me. She delivered this line as though it didn't matter, but they all twitched with interest, because it was what they all wanted to know, what they had all been waiting to hear. This was the only power I had left. I was still the one who decided when we went to my father's salon. Once we were in the salon my power evaporated, because there was nothing I could offer my dad that seemed to interest him any more.

'I don't fancy it,' I said.

'What?' said Sarah.

'Why don't we go to the pub or something,' I said, finishing the vodka.

Polly and Julia soon slipped away. It was dark by the time we walked back up to the high street. We snuck into the pub loos so we could get changed into black miniskirts and denim shirts, so we could redo our eyes and pick the grass out of each other's hair. We found a table, lit cigarettes and soon enough some older boys came to sit with us. We lied and told them we were eighteen, in the last year of A-levels. The boys didn't believe us, but they bought us Bacardi Cokes anyway and there were only two of them and I could just tell that one was interested in Sarah and one was interested in Anya and neither were interested in me, they never were, so instead of enduring the familiar humiliation I left, taking the Tube home, my bag heavy with books and files and uniform that I would never need again.

It was past eleven when I got home. I was surprised to find that Dad wasn't back yet. I shouted out to Mum that I was fine, she should go to sleep, and I slumped on the sofa. I turned on the television, watched whatever was on. The contents of my stomach felt toxic, slopping and steaming, but I didn't have the energy to make myself toast to soak it all up. All I could do was smoke more cigarettes, breathe heavily through my nose, feel my skin alternate between heat and chills, wish I was someone else.

Dad came back later, whistling as he opened the door.

'You're here!' he said. 'Where'd you get to? We had fun, me and the girls. They said they'd seen you, that you were going for it, celebrating finishing your exams, rolling around in the grass, getting high like a nutter, they said!'

He sat down next to me, making me tip into his side of the sofa.

'Which girls,' I mumbled.

Dad had taken the remote control from me and was flicking between channels.

'Which girls?' I said again, wanting to be heard but worried that the effort of speaking too loudly would make me vomit. I was suddenly aware that the sensation had not returned to my limbs, not since turning over the exam paper. I was still just a torso, my chest constricted, my breath short. Maybe I was going to die; maybe tonight was the night.

'Polly and her mate, you know, the one with the nice hair.'

He lit a cigarette and coughed out smoke, a sound like strangled laughter.

'Julia.'

19

2015, London

I used to think I was more happy than sad, but not today. I used to wake up and feel optimistic, even though there was no good reason for it, but not today.

I feel as though I am experiencing all the emotions I have ever suppressed, all the things I have witnessed, all at once. It is as if I am made of wires, blue and red, thousands of them, bunched and knotted. These wires are emotion, memory, twisted to make limbs, a neck, a head, not bone and muscle, that is not what I am made of. It is painful to be made of wire, the broken ends flickering and sharp, everything muddled together and impossible to prise apart so that one memory gets tangled with a different emotion and the overriding emotion and memories dominate everything, all the disappointment and sadness.

I cannot do this by myself any more. I don't want to do this by myself any more.

When I get into work I close the door to my office and write an email to Julia Samuel. I ask if she will counsel me for suppressed grief and trauma. She emails back at once. She is apologetic but for various reasons (she is already counselling someone I know well) she cannot be my therapist. Instead she suggests someone called Fiona.

I send an email to Fiona. I explain that I have never grieved for my dead sister, that I cannot remember my dead sister, and that I am scared of how detached and isolated I have become.

Fiona replies. We arrange the first session.

Fiona's consulting room is on the King's Road, close to where I grew up, close to where Candy and I went to primary school and where Candy and Dad are buried. In our first session I tell her about Candy's death, about how I cannot remember her, how sad this makes me feel, how I have been trying to write about my childhood, how mad I am feeling and how it feels as though all these things are connected.

Fiona has long white hair, a soft Irish accent and a tattoo on her inner wrist. She tells me that my memories are still in my body somewhere, hidden or buried or submerged. We talk about Candy as if she is in a dark cellar, one with a trap door that had been shut, locked, weighted down under the heavy things that have been piled upon it so long ago that the whereabouts of the trap door has been forgotten. We talk about the days, weeks and months following Candy's death, how my family dealt with the tragedy and how the people around us responded to it. I explain how I used all my energy and all my determination to forget her so that I could fit in, so that I could survive the world in which I found myself. I tell her about all the drink and the drugs and the boys, the desperation for oblivion, the destruction of the brain cells that contained Candy.

'I did this to myself.'

'She is still inside you,' Fiona insists.

'Where? How do I find her?'

'Start by looking at photographs. Sit by yourself and let yourself feel any emotions that come up. Sit with the feelings. Put photographs of Candy up around the house, maybe carry one around with you, maybe bring some to the next session and we can look at them together.'

I get home after work, bathe the girls, put them to bed, read them stories, kiss their creaseless brows. They are so flamboyant in sleep, arms slung above their heads. Mike is out, so I make myself an omelette and salad, something quick and easy, and then I go into the living room, shut the door, light a couple of candles, posh ones from work. This is a ritual I am taking seriously.

It is a strange thing to be the person who holds the physical remains of a lost family. My mother still has most of Candy's possessions, but I have everything else, things that were in the flat in Battersea where we grew up, paintings and plant pots, figurines and even Dad's old porn magazines (hidden in a cool bag in a cupboard; I am convinced they will be worth something one day). Sometimes our flat can feel like a museum, each item – candlestick, broken clock, bronze Ganesh – with its own history and emotional power, potent with memory. Perhaps all this stuff should be labelled and put into chronological order too, I think as I survey the mad jumble on the mantelpiece.

But the most important artefact is the family photograph album. We only had one, red leather, gold-embossed cover, thick cardboard pages. The album was used and reused, old pictures taken out, new ones stuck in, captions written in biro which don't refer to the photograph they are next to any more. When we first had it Candy was alive and by the end of it she is dead. The first two-thirds of the album are densely packed with memories, but in the final pages the pictures are loose, yet to be attached, as if we gave up on this impossible business of trying to be a family.

The album is now in my possession, stacked with other albums that I have filled over the years. It is frayed at the spine, there are random black splodges on the red leather, and the gold is almost rubbed away.

I carry the album to the sofa. It weighs heavily on my lap. As I begin to turn the creaking pages I realize that I cannot remember the last time I looked through it. And then I find her. A brown-eyed baby in pink gingham with a dummy around her neck, straining out of the arms that hold her. A little girl in a too-big white woollen cardigan holding a blue plastic lunch box. In a nightie, being hugged by my mother who smiles with her eyes closed, pressing her face to her little girl. Dressed for school, eating Rice Krispies off the glass table. With Dad feeding the ducks in the park; with her Big Yellow Teapot toy on Christmas Day; asleep; on holiday, eating an ice-lolly; holding her nose as she splashes out of the bottom of a slide, just about to hit the water, caught in time and movement. I realize how much she looks like Minna. On the day before Minna was born, when amniotic fluid was trickling out of my cervix, I walked through

Brompton Cemetery to Chelsea and Westminster Hospital trying to jog along the birth. I stopped at the grave where Candy's ashes were buried along with Dad.

'I'm about to have another baby!' I told them.

At the end of the album, among the unstuck photographs, are pictures from our final family holiday in Tunisia. There is a photograph of Candy on a camel, the day before the night when she died, and she is waving and it is as if she is waving goodbye.

I cry and I cry, the sobs wrenching my body. My eyes are raw from crying and the muscles in my cheeks ache.

But the next day I feel as though something I have been holding has been let go, all those tears, waiting to be released, fresh as the day they were made.

In the weeks that follow I try to remember Candy. I sit down and scrunch my face, straining to find the faintest scrap of her. I have a momentary vision of plastic dummies, two or three, strung on bits of ribbon around a child's neck, but other than that, nothing. I try harder, and find that I am starting to animate the photographs of her. At first I am elated, thinking: This is it, this is a memory! But then I realize I have merely fixed an image of her in my brain and made it speak. Many of these pictures were taken when I was not even present, so I know these are false memories.

I go for dinner with my old friend Bella and tell her about what I have been doing. I tell her that I have no memories of Candy.

'But I remember Candy. She was so cheeky. She

was always trying to get into your bedroom when we were in there. You would tell her to go away but sometimes she would just come in anyway and sit on the bed. She drove us mad. I think she just wanted to hang out with us.'

That night I have a dream about Candy.

I cannot remember dreaming about her before.

In the dream I am in a house, on the ground floor. The house belongs to my friend Annabel. It is a place I like and feel safe in.

As I realize it is Annabel's house, Annabel appears.

'What are you doing down here? You are upstairs,' she says.

I am confused by this, so I go up the stairs to find out where I really am. At the top of the stairs there is a closed door. I open it. There is a room. In the room there is a bed and on the bed lies a child. At first I don't know who she is. She looks like she could be mine, but I know this is not Hebe or Minna.

'Who are you?' I ask.

'I am Candy,' she says.

'But you're dead,' I say.

She looks at me as though I am an idiot.

'I'm dead, I'm dead, I'm dead,' she says in a silly high-pitched voice as if she is trying to annoy me. I'm angry with her, and scared too. I want to stuff the words back in her mouth.

When I wake up I'm freaked out. I tell Mike about my dream.

'I'm really glad you have started talking about your sister,' he says. 'It has been so weird for so long.'

Mike is open-hearted; he doesn't keep secrets. When we were first together he would sometimes suggest that we visit the almond tree that my parents had planted in the garden of Candy's school, Bousfield, to commemorate her life. On the anniversary of her death, or on her birthday, he would say, 'Isn't today the day when Candy died?' or 'Isn't today Candy's birthday?' And I would grunt yes, annoyed that he seemed to want me to do something or say something when I had nothing to give. Mike soon stopped mentioning Candy and her special days. He allowed me to go on pretending that nothing was wrong, because that was what I seemed to want.

20

1991, London and Portugal

'One for the road,' said Dad, and he filled Anya's glass with wine which spilt down her nightie when she brought it to her mouth.

It was past midnight and I was tired and drunk but I didn't care because it was more fun to be awake with Dad than to be asleep. We were flying to Portugal in the morning. We would be in a different country by lunchtime, which made staying up and getting drunk feel like something without consequences.

Anya and I shared a single bed and she kicked me in the night so I barely slept.

I had no idea what time it was when Mum woke us, but it was still dark.

'The minicab will be here in twenty minutes,' she said.

Dad listened to his Walkman all the way to the airport, mouthing the words to songs that only he could hear. Mum was in the front with the cab driver, checking her handbag, moving bits of paper with her fingers as though she was doing filing: tickets, passports, cash; tickets, passports, cash.

Dad was still listening to his Walkman when we got on the plane. When I tried to talk to him he shouted 'WHAT?', pointing to his headphones. He started snoring as the plane took off, a jagged exhalation. His lungs were in bad shape; I could hear it. He'd once told me that when he was little his asthma was so bad that his mum often thought he would die. She would lie next to him on the carpet and say, 'Come on, Gavin, breathe, come on, stay with me.'

We walked down the steps from the aeroplane. The air smelt of sunshine and dust.

'We're here!' I said, as if it was some sort of achievement.

We collected our suitcases and Mum found our tour-operator representative, a blonde in a tight red skirt suit who talked about the weather, the food, the nightclubs as the tour bus bounced from side to side on winding foreign roads. When we saw the flat hazy blue of the sea the people on the bus went 'oooh'.

By the time we got to our holiday village the sun was right above us, baking the earth. It was a relief to go into the air-conditioned office. Mum had to sign bits of paper and hand over our passports. Anya sat on a chair, her cheeks blotchy with heat, her eyelids drooping. When Mum was finished Dad leant over the white counter to talk to the receptionist, his heels popping out of his espadrilles.

'Do you have a phone here, my darling? Because there are a couple of work things I need to be keeping tabs on, so I'll be putting in a few calls.'

'Certainly, Senhor 'Odge,' she replied.

Dad pushed a two-thousand-escudo note across the desk.

'What work things?' I asked as we followed a porter dragging our bags along the patchwork stone pathway.

'None of your beeswax,' said Dad.

The minute we were in our room we opened our suitcases and found our swimming costumes. We didn't pull up the blinds or decide who was sleeping in which bed, any of that, all we wanted was to jump into a swimming pool. We ran all the way there. We were bare-footed and the pathway stones were hot enough to cook a pizza on; but that was not why we ran. Once we got to the pool, I kept running around to the deep end. I held my nose and jumped, falling deep into the cool blue.

When we finally got out of the pool again we found that Dad had established himself on a lounger in full sunlight. He had a beer and a packet of fags. I asked him for money so we could have beer and cigarettes too, as well as ice-cream.

'Where's Mum?'

'She's gone to the supermarket. You know what she's like.'

We found two loungers with a good view of the pool so we could eat our ice-creams and look for handsome boys from behind our sunglasses.

Mum already had the washing machine going when we got back to the villa. I had no idea what she was washing, seeing as we had only just arrived.

'I'm having a shower,' I shouted.

'Good girl,' she shouted back.

I lay on my bed in my wet towel, making my clean

white sheets damp, smoking a cigarette, tapping ash into a water glass. The patio doors were open and there were already three flies circling. Anya was asleep.

Later, we shared the small rectangular mirror to put on make-up before we went out. My face was pink from the sun and glowed with grease so I had to use a lot of bronzer to create a matte effect, which made my face a different shade to the rest of my body. But still, I thought I looked OK, bright blonde hair and dark eyebrows, nothing really matching.

The sky was the colour of a peach and we followed a sandy path to a seafront restaurant. We sat outside, a low bamboo fence separating us from the beach. There was sand on the concrete floor and I could hear the fizzing sound the sea made each time it receded. Dad put on a Spanish accent to speak to the waiter, even though we were in Portugal.

'Vino bianco, per favor, uno bottilio.'

I drank quickly. The cold, green wine quenched my thirst. Dad got drunk quickly too. We were the same like that. I ordered clams, and he had mussels. He did this thing with them, inserting his tongue between the little coral-coloured flaps and making sexy noises; he did it each time, with each mussel; he wouldn't stop and I laughed because I thought it was funny.

'Gavin, don't,' said Mum, and there was an edge to her voice, but he didn't stop, and telling him to stop was the worst thing to do, because it only made him do it more. Even I knew that.

*

Anya and I were in our separate beds. The lights were off; the sound of Dad's snoring rumbled through the villa like a train.

'God, that thing your dad did with the mussels was disgusting,' said Anya.

I didn't speak. There was a cold feeling under my skin. It was the feeling I got when I suddenly realized I had missed something, got something wrong, not understood. I knew that there was something fucked up about me and it was not even my fault, but I would never be able to put it right.

'I know,' I said. 'Gross.'

We lay on bathroom towels on the weird bouncy foreign grass in the patch of garden outside our room. We had everything we needed: Walkmen, tapes, magazines, books, a hairbrush, bottles of water, snacks, nail varnish, tweezers. I was using oil and lemon juice instead of suntan lotion because that was what Dad was using. I wanted to get really brown. I wanted to get more brown than Anya, who was freckly and pink. I wanted to be brown when we got back to school in two weeks, so that everyone would know I had been away and that I was the sort of person who got really brown. My skin was tight but that was good because it meant it was happening.

Mum was also at the villa, in her bit of garden.

'Gavanndra!'

She called for me, and at first when I stood up I felt I might faint because I was so hot. I drank some warm water from a plastic bottle that felt soft, as if it was melting.

'Gavanndra!'

'I'm coming.'

'Do my back, will you?'

I rubbed my mum's wide back with factor 15 suntan cream. There were moles and tiny pink blobs on her skin.

'Do it properly, rub it in, I can still feel the cream on me,' she said when I stopped too soon. I didn't like that her back was sweaty and there was a deep pit where a mole had been removed a couple of years before.

'Do you want me to do you? You're looking quite red.'

'No, thanks.'

My father had a theory that in order to get a really deep and long-lasting tan it was important to burn away the top layers of skin on the first couple of days of a holiday, and then you could start tanning the fresh new skin beneath. So at the end of the day we helped him by tugging the peeling skin from his back. It came off in satisfying sheets, like clingfilm, which we scrunched into small grey rags. Normally I would have found this fun, but I was in too much pain; my back and my chest were the worst, the skin felt tender and hot, as if it was still cooking.

'I'll get the bath going,' said Mum.

'Have a beer while you are getting in, it will make it easier,' said Dad.

My father had another theory, or perhaps this theory was my mother's, that the best way to treat sunburn was to get into a bath, the hotter the better, as hot as was bearable, and this would take the sting out of the burn.

I lowered myself into the bath slowly, thighs, bottom,

My mum, Jan Hodge (or Jan Burdette, as she was known then), when she was a model. Here posing on a Citroen DS. Early seventies.

Mum and Dad, Gavin Hodge, on their wedding day. Dad had forgotten to buy Mum a birthday present, so he married her as a surprise treat at the Chelsea Registry office on the Kings Road. July 1975.

Mum and me outside our local pub in the World's End, Chelsea. Summer, 1975.

Dad in Marbella. He'd gone there to attempt to stop taking heroin. He succeeded, but it didn't last long. Summer 1979.

Me and Mum in the flat in
Chelsea, before Candy was born.
Mum told me that she and Dad
were so out of it most of the time
that they were surprised to
discover they were pregnant a
second time. Late seventies.

Me, Maranda and baby Candy at my
Hodge grandparents' house in
Chislehurst. 1979.

Me, Maranda and Dad at the
flat in Battersea. As a child
and a young woman Maranda
always felt rejected by Dad.
Early eighties.

My mum and Maranda's mum,
Kerstin Widlund, both blonde
models, both alcoholics. My dad
clearly had a type. Late seventies.

Me and my mum, while she was still modelling
(attempts were made to make me a child model,
which failed). Late seventies.

Candy Hodge, posing. Early eighties.

Me, Dad and Candy in Jamaica. Dad paid for this luxury trip by selling his life story to the *News of the World*. The series was called 'The Shampoo Seducer' and in it he claimed to have slept with 1,000 women in one busy year. Summer 1980.

Me, Mum, Candy and Candy's godfather, Andy Pierce, in the flat in Battersea. This is the living room where the junkies would congregate most evenings. Early eighties.

Me and Candy in sunny Chislehurst, where my Hodge grandparents lived in suburban splendour. Early eighties.

Me, Candy and my half-sister, Maranda Widlund, during one of Maranda's rare trips to the UK. According to my mum, Maranda was the one who decked us out in tinsel, showing an early flair for fashion and hair styling. Early eighties.

Me, aged about eight, in the white nightie I used to wear to sit with the junkies in the sitting room after dark, in my parents' bedroom in the flat in Battersea. Early eighties.

Candy on a camel ride in Tunisia. This is one of the last photographs we have of her. She died that night. April 1989.

Me, aged fourteen, in Tunisia. After five years of relative normality I was doing well and thriving at school, but that was all about to come to an abrupt end. April 1989.

Me, aged sixteen, just two years later, after Candy had died. I was going to Dad's basement salon in Knightsbridge after school most evenings to take drugs and drink away the sadness and confusion. 1991.

Me and Dad at Pucci Pizza restaurant on the King's Road, where we spent many a drunken and druggie night. Early nineties.

Me and Dad outside the pub on Beauchamp Place, Knightsbridge, where we would go drinking. Early nineties.

Me and Dad on my wedding day in Devon. Dad did my hair, got very stoned and delivered a speech that had the whole marquee laughing. September 2006.

Me in the Hanover Square offices of *Tatler* magazine, where I worked as deputy editor and acting editor for five years. This picture was taken as publicity for the BBC documentary *Posh People: Inside Tatler.* 2014.

Me, Maranda, her daughter Biba and her friend, the actress Britt Ekland, taken at a launch party for a photography exhibition in Los Angeles. February 2017.

Biba and Hebe, cousins and firm friends. Here they are on Biba's first English summer holiday, enjoying the slot machines on the pier at Southwold, Suffolk. August 2017.

Mike, Hebe and Minna. February 2020.

Some of the contents of Candy's box, containing all the precious things that my parents could not bear to throw away after she died in 1989, opened again for the first time by me and my mum in 2019.

tummy, and then my back, chest and upper arms. I did not breathe while I did this, it hurt too much, my skin sizzling on contact with the water. I drank the beer in short, breathless gulps. I had to remain in the bath until the water cooled to body temperature because this was the method. I had recently learnt that this was also a method used to cook white fish. I shouted for someone to bring me another bottle of beer but no one came.

I felt triumphant when I emerged from the bathroom, slick with aftersun, a towel coiled around my head, but Dad had gone and there was no one to congratulate me.

'Where is he?' I asked.

My first ever sentence was 'Where's Daddy?'

Mum was sitting on the green leather sofa; she was alone in the living room, which smelt of Dad's cigarettes and aftershave. She was dressed up to go out, fresh make-up and nail varnish, and for some reason it made me sad that she was just waiting by herself, not doing anything, smoking a cigarette or having a drink or even reading a magazine.

'He's gone to make a call, a work thing.'

'What work thing?' I asked.

'I don't know, darling, I didn't ask. Go and get dressed, will you, or we'll be late.'

After dinner at the same place, where we all ate the same food we'd had the night before, except Anya, who had pizza, we walked to the shore to look at the sea. There was a full moon, bright and heavy. It made a rippling stripe of silver on the black sea.

'Isn't that beautiful, man, look at that,' said Dad. He was excited, bouncing in his espadrilles. 'There was this one time, in Marbella with Kerstin. I took some acid and it was a full moon, just like this one, and I realized that if I could just walk along the silver path I would actually get to the moon. So I started walking, right into the sea. When I got nearly up to my neck Kerstin started shouting. She didn't really speak English, so I couldn't understand a word. She followed me out into the sea, dragged me back to the beach, really messed with my trip . . .'

We didn't say anything.

'So I never did get to walk on the fucking moon,' he said, laughing, flicking his cigarette into the water.

On the next day we kept out of the sun for the morning. Instead I walked to the office on my own. It was mid-morning and Anya was having one of her naps. I wanted to make sure everything was organized for me to make the call the next day. My old babysitter Elaine was getting to the flat at 3 p.m. her time to open the envelope with my GCSE results. I remembered my Latin exam, how I'd felt when I turned over that paper. Why does shock always feel cold, never hot? I thought as I entered the cold air-conditioned office with the desk, the chair, the little pamphlets about water slides, donkey parks and museums devoted to the local fortified wine, the sorts of thing we never did on holiday because it might interfere with the tanning schedule.

I heard his voice first, murmuring and intimate. I let

the door close quietly behind me and then I looked. He was on the telephone, one elbow on the desk, shuffling his hips just a little, tapping his foot, always fidgeting.

'I can't stop thinking about you,' he said. He was stroking the desk with his index finger, just as I'd seen him stroke the soft underside of Julia's forearm on one of the evenings we'd all spent together. She'd become a regular fixture in the last month, never invited by me; she and Polly would just turn up. Dad had been more manic than ever, showing off, spending money he didn't have, taking us all to the posh bar at the end of Beauchamp Place for honey-glazed sausages and champagne that came in buckets filled with ice, sitting in a velvet upholstered corner with young girls squeezed in on either side, not being discreet about taking cocaine, three of us going up to the loo together. It was fun and decadent and crazy and I would make myself feel sick by eating too much and drinking too much, so would try to sober up with the coke, and then when I began to feel flat and strange I would tell Dad I wanted to go home, and he would say, 'You mustn't go, that would be boring,' and we all knew that boring was the worst thing anyone could be. So I drank more, snorted more, and pretended that it was fun and brilliant, pretended that I was having the best time in the world.

I felt the area between my ribs go numb. I knew that this was not where my heart was but it felt like my heart. I stood behind him. I made my blood slow and still, my breath imperceptible, so he wouldn't know I was behind him. The receptionist looked at me, and I returned her gaze.

'Just get the flight. I'll sort everything out. It's so beautiful here, you'll love it. You need a break. I need to see you.'

The receptionist coughed and rolled her eyes so Dad would realize that someone was behind him.

'I've got to go . . . Yes, yes . . . OK, me too.'

He put down the phone and turned around. He was holding himself like a boxer, muscles tense, one foot in front of the other, ready for anything, for anyone, ready for a fight. Perhaps he thought it was Mum.

'Oh, it's only you,' he said when he saw me.

Fuck you, I thought.

I didn't say that, though.

'Who were you talking to?' I said.

I knew the answer, of course. It had been obvious all along. What an idiot I'd been. How they must have laughed at me.

'Julia. Come on, I'll buy you an ice-cream.' He laid a couple of escudo notes on the desk. 'Thank you, my darling.'

'OK, Senhor 'Odge.'

He walked past me, pushing open the doors to the office, letting in the hot air, sauntering into the sun as if nothing had happened, as if he hadn't even noticed the jagged crack in the universe that had just opened between us.

At first I couldn't move. I felt as though I hadn't moved for such a long time. But he was leaving without even checking to see that I was following so I shook myself free.

'I don't want an ice-cream,' I said when I caught up with him.

'What! Are you going on a diet?'

'No, I'm not going on a diet.'

'But you have put on a bit.'

'I'm not as fat as you.'

Dad didn't answer. We walked along the path between the hedges, heading for the pool. He lit a cigarette and handed it to me; then he lit one for himself. I dragged the hot smoke into my lungs. I still couldn't feel anything.

We got to the pool bar and Dad pulled up a stool for me and one for himself. He ordered two beers and two whiskies.

'Have you ever had a chaser?' he asked.

'No.'

'You do it like this,' he said.

And even though I hated him, I copied him. A shot of whisky to sting the throat, followed by a cool beer to soothe it.

'What's going on?' I asked.

'Duo mas, Pedro,' Dad shouted, putting two fingers up, in case the handsome waiter, who was not called Pedro or Pablo but Alex, and who spoke very good English with an American accent, had not understood. Alex nodded and smiled.

'Listen, G, remember what I asked you before? The favour. I really want you to think about doing this for me. Tell Mum that you have invited Julia out here, that you want her to come for the second week. There's that spare room. It's no skin off your nose. Don't be a meanie.'

*

It had been one night in the pub back in June, after Mum had booked the holiday, just me and him sitting at the bar.

'Why don't you invite Julia to Portugal? It will be fun to have more people,' he'd said.

'But she's not even my friend.'

'What are you talking about? She's great. And she's having a shitty time at home. It would be a nice thing for you to do to invite her out.'

'I am not inviting Julia to Portugal. There are a million people I would invite on holiday before I would invite her.'

'Fair enough. I've got to go, I've got a client,' he'd said and he slid off his stool and left me at the bar, with his half-drunk beer and his half-smoked cigarette.

'No,' I said.

There was silence between us. I could hear the sounds of people splashing in the pool, the music from the bar stereo, the whirring of a coffee machine, the low hum of the fridge, two people close by having a conversation about football.

Dad sucked his cigarette.

'Are you fucking her?' I asked.

He didn't answer straightaway which meant that he had slept with her, he was sleeping with her.

'What are you talking about? We're in love.'

I put my hands against the bar to steady myself. I got down off the stool. I walked away from him, back to the villa. I did not cry.

Anya was inside, on her bed, reading a magazine,

holding one of those small plastic battery-operated fans to her face.

'Hi,' I said, trying to sound normal.

'Hi,' she replied.

Later that afternoon Mum opened the door to our room. I'd been half asleep.

'Don't wear your jeans tonight, we are going somewhere different, a nice restaurant in Vale do Lobo,' she said.

'Why?'

'We want to do something special for you both, to celebrate your GCSE results.'

'But we don't get them until tomorrow.'

'Don't be pedantic.'

I wore my jeans, a grey T-shirt and my espadrilles. I didn't brush my hair. I was getting dreadlocks in the back. Anya wore a flappy floral dress and redid her liquid eyeliner twice because she couldn't make both sides match.

Mum didn't say anything when she saw me; she just pursed her lips and looked away.

'Is that what you are wearing, Chubbs?' said Dad.

'Yes.'

He looked at Anya. 'You look gorgeous,' he said.

'Let's go,' said Mum.

'Make sure you've got your Gold Card, Jan, this one is going to be expensive,' said Dad.

It was a beautiful evening, I couldn't help but notice that, even though I was so full of rage. We sat outside on a stone terrace. Men in red waistcoats flapped large napkins on to our laps. Pergolas were draped with blooming jasmine and fat candles burned with still flames because there was no breeze. The warm air hung heavy about our shoulders and made us glow.

'Order whatever you want, girls, you only live once,' said Dad.

I scanned the menu, looking for the most expensive thing.

'Chateaubriand,' I said. I didn't know what this was, but it cost more than anything else.

'Brill, we'll share,' said Dad.

And even though I hated him, I was finding it hard to keep my hate stoked in this pretty place with the nice wine and tasty food, and I knew that I was shallow, but that was not my fault.

The bill came and Dad didn't even look at it; he just blew luxurious smoke rings and finished off the last of the wine while Mum examined it and, with a small sigh, put down her credit card.

That night I could not sleep. I took Anya's fan from her bedside table and stood outside looking up at the moon and holding the fan to my face until the battery ran out.

The next day was the hottest yet. There was no breeze. The fat green leaves on the bushes had lost their juicy lustre; the gravel on the pathway was molten with heat. We walked to the pool for waffles and a swim, Anya smoking a cigarette, the paper burning down quicker than usual.

We sat under the awning by the bar, although I made

sure my chair was in the sun. Dad was sprawled on a sun lounger nearby; his skin a glossy walnut brown, the yellow of his Walkman bright against his belly.

I realized I had forgotten my suntan oil. Hawaiian Tropic, factor 5. There was no way I was going to use Anya's factor 30.

'I am just going back, order a waffle for me,' I said.

The air around the villa seemed to shimmer and warp. It was so hot that the birds had stopped singing.

I went in through the door to the kitchen. The dishes were only half finished. The washing machine was not on. It was weirdly quiet. Then I heard a gulping, sniffing noise. Mum was crying.

I went into the sitting room.

Mum was on the sofa in her huge blue kaftan, her bare feet on the floor, wide apart, toenails painted pink, elbows on her knees. She was holding a piece of paper. The paper was lined, torn out of a schoolbook. I recognized the handwriting: it was round and childish, done in purple felt-tip pen, fat hearts instead of dots over each 'i'.

I was good in an emergency. I was able to make myself cold and distant; I was able to react without emotion while other people panicked. It was an ability that I cultivated.

'Mum,' I said.

She looked at me. 'Did you know about this?' she asked, waving the piece of paper in my direction.

'No.'

I was not lying. I did not know about the note.

'It's a . . .' Mum paused, looked back down, read the

words again. 'It's a love letter, written by one of your friends to your father.'

'Which one? Which one of my friends?'

I was lying now. I knew who had written the letter.

'Julia. I met her once. Down at the salon. While you were in Italy. I did wonder what she was doing there while you were away . . .'

'She's not my friend,' I said.

'Well, then how did he meet her if you didn't introduce them?'

How deep was the betrayal – that was what she wanted to know. Both of you, or just him.

I could feel myself getting angry. I hadn't done anything wrong. Everything wrong had been done to me.

'She's not my friend. She's friends with Polly.'

'But you knew about it. He tells you everything. You must have known.'

Mum started crying again. I was stuck to the floor. I couldn't help her. I didn't know how. Eventually Mum stopped.

'Get him for me.'

Everything could change in a moment and I was inside one of those moments.

'Where have you been?' asked Anya. The cream had melted on my waffle, making a pool of white.

I ignored her, walking past her to my father.

I knelt down next to him and yanked a headphone out of his ear. Pop.

'Bloody hell. What?'

'Mum found the stupid letter from Julia. She wants to see you.'

He looked at me. 'What did you tell her?'

'For fuck's sake. Nothing.'

He looked at the pool, at the people in their bikinis and shorts, having fun, laughing, eating, splashing. He drank from his bottle of beer. He put the headphone back in his ear, stood up and walked away.

I remained crouched down for a moment. Then I stretched myself out on his lounger and tilted my face up to the sun with my eyes closed. Soon enough a shadow passed over my face.

'What is going on?' asked Anya.

'I think my parents are going to divorce.'

'Oh . . . Shit,' she said.

'Mum found a letter from Julia to Dad, a love letter. Mum was reading it when I went over there just now.'

I sat up, took a swig of Dad's beer. It was warm and unpleasant.

'Shall we go and see what's happening?'

I didn't reply, but Anya started off in the direction of the villa, so I followed.

'I don't remember what it was like when my parents divorced, I was too little,' Anya said as we walked. The sprinklers had been left on for the day, it was that hot. 'But now I can't imagine them ever being together. It'll be the same for you soon, you'll see.'

'But what if he ends up with Julia?'

'Imagine if they get married and have children. She

would be your stepmother! Her children would be your brothers and sisters!'

Anya laughed and I hadn't meant it as a joke.

We got to the villa. I could hear my parents shouting through the closed doors.

'I deserve better than this!'

I couldn't stand it. I couldn't listen to it. It felt too much like that other day, everything collapsing, and all the while the sun shines and the pool sparkles and the tanned people in their swimsuits are laughing because they can't see the devastation because it is not happening to them.

'I'm going to the beach,' I said.

I ran along the path, pulling off my clothes as I went. I walked into the sea, pushing my way through the water; I walked until the water came up to my chest, then I plunged in, my eyes tight shut, my face in the salt water, the safest place to cry. I dissolved into the sea, I couldn't feel my edges, I didn't want to, I was all water.

When I couldn't hold my breath any more I shot up out of the sea, panting, breath ripping my lungs, water streaming from my eyes. I stood there for such a long time, swaying in the water, that my shoulders and chest and face dried to a tight dusting of salt. Nothing had changed: the sun, the beach, the heat, the wetness of the sea, everything was the same; nothing had changed except me. I dragged myself out of the water and sat on the wet shore.

Anya found me. She brought all the things we would need for a day on the beach: towels, sun cream, magazines, water, sunglasses. I lay on my front to read my book and after a while I found that I was able to be myself again.

'It was ridiculous that my mum and dad were ever together in the first place. It was amazing they stayed together this long,' I said.

They weren't suited, never were; apart from the drugs and the alcohol all they had in common was me and my sister, now just me. And I wasn't enough. Never had been. They had only really started trying to be parents when Candy arrived. And then she was gone.

We ate lunch at the beach bar: beer and chips and an omelette, and the beer was cold and the chips were salty, and I thought, I'm alive, aren't I, things aren't so bad, they could always be worse. You have done this before, I thought, picked yourself up and got on with things.

The door to the office swung shut behind me.

'I need to make a call to London,' I said to the receptionist.

'You too, eh!'

I ignored this comment and took the phone. I dialled the number for home. It rang. Elaine picked up.

'Hi, it's me,' I said.

'Oh, hello! Is it nice out there?'

'Yes.'

'Great, well, the weather here has been really bad, so you're lucky to be away.'

'Yeah. Do you have the envelope?'

'Sure, I've got it right here. I've already opened it. Do you want to know your results?'

'Yes, please.'

'Don't worry, they're really good.'

I smiled, closed my eyes. I'd got away with it. Thank God.

'OK.'

'So, you got three As, which is amazing . . .'

There was an icy clamp around my skull. Only three As. She kept talking. Three Bs, three Cs and a D. Cs in Chemistry and Latin. I had been predicted As in everything, I was meant to be doing Latin and Chemistry at A-level. This was the only thing I was any good at. I wasn't pretty and I wasn't sporty and my parents weren't rich and that was the least of it. Clever was all I had. Clever was meant to be my way out; but I had lost that too, along the way.

'Thanks,' I said, my voice whispery. 'See you soon.'

I put down the phone as quickly as I could, Elaine still speaking, saying something pointless and kind.

Mum was in the villa, cleaning her room. Dad was in the spare bedroom, the one he had wanted Julia to stay in. Mum was arranging her possessions, spreading herself out so it didn't feel as if someone was missing. We kept having to do this.

I told her my results.

'But, Gavanndra, that's not what you expected, was it?'

'No,' I said. I was sitting on the edge of the bed. Mum had taken off all the sheets and put them in the machine to wash them clean.

21

2015, London

Fiona and I begin a process called Eye Movement Desensitization and Reprocessing (EMDR – Fiona had just had the training). The first thing I have to do is try to recall every traumatizing experience I've ever had and then score each one out of ten for how anxious and scared it still makes me feel. I fill out a piece of paper printed with a grid of small rectangular boxes: one box for the memory, another for how it makes me feel, another for its score. The memory of watching my sister die in a hotel room in Tunisia scores a ten. The fear, the horror, the numbness in my body is still as fresh as the night I saw it happen. Watching my dad run his finger up and down Julia's soft white inner arm, his sly smile, that scores an eight.

I need an extra piece of paper because I have such a large number of traumatizing memories.

'Is it normal to have so many?' I ask.

'What do you want me to say?' replies Fiona.

'That I am special?'

She laughs.

EMDR is meant to help people process trauma. It eases the passage of 'trapped' trauma out of the body and into memory, so the trauma finally becomes the past and not a constantly relived present.

I sit in a comfy chair opposite Fiona while she moves a small black wand from left to right in a rhythmic fashion. While my eyes flick from side to side, following the wand, I try to remember a specific moment of a traumatic experience. How it felt the moment I walked into the room where my sister was dying, for instance. I try to recall what I saw, the feeling of the carpet under my feet, of my heart thudding in my chest, of the numbness spreading from my fingers up my arms. I watch the wand. Sometimes my eyes go misty and sometimes my memory goes misty too. Fiona stops, asks me what I saw, what I felt, where in my body I felt it, and then we resume. This goes on for a whole session, a tiny moment explored for fifty minutes, a tiny moment that changed a whole life.

'Think of it like watching something from the windows of a train,' Fiona explains.

We repeat this process with many of my memories: the memory of pinching out candles as my father and his junkie friends lay unconscious on the carpet; the memory of my father holding his head thinking he was about to die the morning he was meant to be taking me to the zoo. Sometimes I worry, as I am remembering, that I am not remembering a real moment, but how I have told and been told the incident over the years. Memories have been reshaped, developed, influenced. Sometimes all I have is the taste of butterscotch or the feel of cashmere against my cheek. Some of my memories are images, a moment caught in a flash and burnt on to my brain like a photograph, still there when I close my eyes, decades later. Some of my memories are like houses with rooms where I can walk around, pick things up, put them down. Some of my memories have become five-thousand-word stories. I worry that the EMDR may not work because I am getting confused between what really happened and my remaking of what really happened.

'Is it still real if it has become a story?' I ask Fiona.

'What is real is how it makes you feel,' she says.

At nine fifty I wipe the tears from my face, put on fresh make-up and get the Tube to work.

Sometimes after a session of EMDR I am so exhausted that I have to give up, leave my desk, go home and sleep for hours. But when I come to examine my feelings I find that the memory of watching my sister die scores only six out of ten. Its horror is still a ten, but the way it makes me feel is different, less raw, more distant, something that happened over two decades ago. The aim is to get the score to a two, or even a one.

After a few weeks of this process I find I have the courage to do something I have been too scared to do for twenty-five years: read the diary entry that I made just after Candy died. I wrote the entry in a shiny pink A4 notebook. This notebook has moved with me from flat to flat, packed and unpacked with all my other diaries and books, but never reopened.

I wait for the next time I am alone at home. I get up on to a chair to pull the notebook down from the top shelf where I put it ten years ago. I blow away the cob-webs and the soft grey dust. I take the notebook into the living room. I turn the pages slowly, reverentially, like an archivist examining an ancient manuscript. I feel as if I should be wearing thin white gloves.

I find the entry and read it. The raw immediacy of it is so intense it feels as though someone is grabbing under my sternum, twisting and pulling. Here is the truth. Here is what happened. A report not a recollection. Dangerous. I lay my hand on my chest and try to calm myself. That doesn't work so I make myself a strong vodka and tonic. It tastes good. I drink it fast and make myself another. With semi-drunkenness comes familiar and welcome relaxation in my mind and my limbs.

'You've done something brave. You should be proud of yourself,' I say to myself.

It is only when I wake up the next morning, a little hungover, that it occurs to me I have found out some-thing new about Candy. It was there in my diary entry: 'One of the people said that Candy looked like me and she was happy.'

I make myself reread again and again the words that I cannot remember writing about a moment I cannot remember happening.

My sister, there on the page.

22

16 April 1989

Dear Diary,

*My sister Candida Meander Hodge died on Tuesday 4th April
at approximately 4.30 in the morning. She was nine years old. It
was in Tunisia. That night she had been fine. I remember Anya
and I were sitting around the pool table with some friends we
had made and Candy came over. One of the people said that
Candy looked like me and she was happy.*

   *That night she had danced with daddy for the first time ever.
Before she went to bed she complained of a sore throat. At 4
mummy came into my room and asked for some Strepsils – she
said Candy had a bad cough. Mummy left and I could hear
Candy coughing and whooping. I then heard daddy shout
'Candy, no!' So I screamed and ran into their bedroom. Candy
was sitting on the bed limp. She had stopped breathing. Daddy
was shouting 'Candy, no' continually and trying to give her the
kiss of life. I ran down the corridor to the main hall where
mummy was trying to get the staff to call the doctor or
something. So I ran back. Candy was now on the floor and she
was coughing up blood. But at least I thought she was breathing
again. Then they carried her to the taxi that was waiting to*

take her to the hospital. Daddy and mummy and I believe that Candy died here in the hotel in daddy's arms.

That night was a horrendous nightmare which I don't want to remember.

23

2015, London

Every time I talk to Fiona, when I pause or look away or my throat catches, she asks: 'Where do you feel this?' I tell her the place and she then puts her hand on wherever it is – her stomach, her throat, her sternum – as if she is trying to get me to do the same thing, to really feel it, and then perhaps to let it go.

Fear and grief are trapped in my body and Candy has lost her body (she was not reincarnated as a rabbit). It seems that I have to get out of my mind and get into my body.

I try a fascial-release massage which is meant to unlock blocked emotions. I change into paper pants in a narrow treatment room in Harrods so a sixty-year-old Frenchwoman can knead and pinch me relentlessly. When she gets to my right hamstring she grabs a fistful of flesh and pulls and pulls, as if she is trying to pull it off. ''Ere is the trauma!' she says triumphantly, and pulls harder. I am so bruised afterwards.

I visit a craniosacral therapist in Harley Street who specializes in post-traumatic body work. She makes me relive, moment by moment, the night my sister died, stopping me every few moments to make me look at the carpet, the wall, so that my body understands that I am safe and not in that place any more. She explains how animals go still when they are afraid, and once the threat is gone, they quiver and shake the fear out of their bodies. 'Which is why animals don't suffer from PTSD,' she says. Then I lie on a treatment bed and she cradles my skull, pressing lightly into its base. Afterwards I feel blurry and subtly altered.

I find two acupuncturists: one handsome and brilliant, who was drawn to acupuncture after the death of his father and specializes in grief (although the first points he treats me for are shock); and another who is brilliant in different ways, whom I do not see for grief, but for stress and wrinkles. I do not tell her about my sister, my childhood, anything. She just assumes I am someone with a smart job who is a bit anxious and a bit vain.

Laura's speciality is facial acupuncture, which involves many tiny needles being inserted into the face to prevent lines and sagging. When Laura finishes inserting the needles, she always says 'Now I am going to work with your energy' and stands next to me with her hands hovering over my chest or abdomen. I close my eyes and I see colours and shapes which sometimes coalesce into faces, sometimes I even hear voices. I feel heat moving around my body or concentrating in one spot, like the sun being focused through a magnifying glass. Afterwards I always ask Laura what she has been doing, how the reiki works, but she can't really explain.

I book an appointment with her because the psoriasis on my lips is not getting any better.

'Oh yes, I can see,' says Laura.

'I've been using steroid cream, but I know that's bad. I had to lie to the pharmacist to get them to sell it to me, tell them it was for my elbows!' I say, laughing, wanting to be funny and likeable, but Laura doesn't even smile.

I am, by this point, lying on the treatment bed in my black bra and black pants, two towels arranged over my body, a heavy beige blanket over the towels, weighing me down, forcing me to be still. Laura has already inserted four needles, two into the points between my big toe and the next one, and two more in the points behind my inner ankle bones. I am looking forward to the one that goes in my forehead; it's like an off button, shutting down my over-active brain. Laura's hands hover over my face, as though she is trying to decide where to place the next needle. She seems distracted, flustered even.

'I'm sorry, but there's someone here,' she says.

I lift my head, expecting to see someone else in the room. I often reflect on the careless vulnerability of the therapy room; anything could happen to you, lying down virtually naked with your eyes shut.

There is no one. No one that I can see.

Laura turns up the lights. She looks at the empty black chair next to the display case containing her collection of crystals. 'She's very naughty, very agitated,' she says.

Laura turns to me. 'Was there ever anyone in your life who really liked sweets? She smells of sweets. It's a very strong smell.'

Ever anybody? It takes me a moment to work out what she means.

'I . . .'

I stumble over what to say.

'Stop it, just stop that now,' says Laura, but not to me. 'She's so jumpy. She seems frustrated. She doesn't know what happened to her. You really don't know who this could be?'

Of course I know who this could be.

I look at Laura, look at the chair. The air in the room feels heavy, weighted, or perhaps it is just me under the blanket.

'I think it might be my sister,' I say. 'She liked sweets. She died suddenly when she was nine years old. We were on holiday in Tunisia. She contracted a virus, a very rare one, only one child in Europe gets it every year, on average. It shut down all her vital organs. When she went to sleep she was fine, but when she woke up in the middle of the night she was very unwell and she died.'

It is the story I tell when I have to, when someone asks me if I have any siblings and I don't have the heart to say no, or they aren't satisfied with 'It's complicated'. It's the story I'm able to tell without my voice cracking. I don't know if the rarity thing is true, but it was something my mother told me, probably because I was so scared. What she was really telling me was that it was impossible for what happened to my sister to happen to me; and so that is what I tell other people when the subject comes up, which it does not often. I am trying to stop them feeling afraid, for themselves and for their children, just as my mother did with me. The story is an act of kindness, and now here I am being kind to Laura.

She inserts a needle in my forehead.

'You need to tell her what happened. You need to talk to her.'

I think about this for a moment. It sounds very strange. But not dangerous.

'Do I need to talk to her out loud?' I ask, feeling self-conscious.

'In your head is fine, if that is how you want to do it. But I can't be in this room any more. I'm really sorry; it's too much for me. I feel like I can't breathe.'

Laura turns down the lights and leaves quickly.

The thought that this is very irregular does cross my mind. But I trust Laura, I like her, and it is kind of incredible. Laura had no idea that I had a dead sister, and yet here she is telling me that Candy is in the room and is upset because she doesn't know what happened to her.

I make myself comfortable.

'Come here, Candy, come on, let me hug you. I am here. I am so sorry that I haven't been, but I am here now. Come to me. I know you are scared and confused – it all happened so suddenly, didn't it, out of the blue, none of us knew what was happening, we were all scared.'

I don't know if I am doing it right, but I keep going. I try to imagine a child sitting on the chair, kicking legs that do not reach the floor. I imagine her biting the tip of her thumb and then sliding off the chair, walking towards me, climbing up on to the bed and into my arms. I imagine the weight of a child on my body, the way my own children feel when they lie on me, sprawling and heavy.

177

'It's OK, calm down.'

I imagine stroking her silky hair.

'I'll tell you what I know. You caught a virus, a virus is a thing that attacks your body from the inside, and that's what it was doing all that time we were on holiday, but we didn't know it. While you were playing in the pool it was growing, and then that night it grew so big and strong that it was able to start attacking. It attacked all the important things inside you, your lungs, your liver, so you couldn't breathe and then your heart stopped, and that is how it killed you. You died in that hotel bedroom with me and Dad. I am so sorry there was nothing I could do. I am so sorry I could not save you.'

And I find that I am crying and I hug her even tighter.

'We loved you so much. We still do. And we needed you so much. We all fell apart after you died.'

And something inside me shifts and relaxes, or perhaps it is Candy who relaxes, because now she knows what happened, because now her sister, whom she always looked up to, who has been ignoring her all these years, has spoken to her once more, hugged her, remembered her, told her she loves her.

'I am so sorry,' I say inside my head and I stroke her hair.

I hear footsteps. Laura re-enters the room.

'That's better,' she says, and she takes the needles from my feet, my ankles, my forehead.

24

1991, London

Putney was not far away from Battersea, but I had never been there before and it felt very foreign to me that afternoon, street after street of boring Victorian red-brick houses. I couldn't quite believe that he'd ended up here. I couldn't quite believe any of it. The pavement underfoot felt soft when it should have been hard; the buildings shimmered as though they might disintegrate; nothing seemed real.

Somewhere inside I was anxious, excited, scared, sad. But those feelings seemed very faint, and mostly I just felt blank, I was here now, I might as well get on with it, one foot in front of the other, yes, here it is, number 39, flat 2, ring the bell, wait for him to answer, wait to hear his voice again.

'G, is that you? Come on up.'

It had been four weeks since Mum had thrown him out. I'd told him I never wanted to see him again. But the hate bloomed in me, full and furious, and then it dispersed and I found I still loved him, after everything. I couldn't help it.

I walked up the stairs, feet heavy, not thinking about anything, thinking about everything. I stood outside the door. It was painted dark red. I lifted my hand, made a fist, knocked once. He must have been waiting on the other side, because he opened it straightaway.

'Hello, my darling!' he said.

He was bouncing on the balls of his feet. I leant forward to kiss him on the cheek and he grabbed me, hugged me. My face was squashed against his soft cashmere jumper and I couldn't breathe.

'You've lost weight, girl, you feel all bony,' he said as he released me.

'You don't,' I said, and I walked around him like an angry cat, through the hallway and into the living room.

So this was where our home had gone.

Here were all the things he had taken. The terracotta bowl in the shape of a hand where he kept his change, the brass Moroccan plate, the video recorder and the videos, some of them my recordings with my handwriting on the labels, *Time Bandits, Excalibur, The Man Who Fell to Earth*. I had been there when he had taken these items, sitting in my room with 'Stay Free' by the Clash turned up loud so that I wouldn't be able to hear what was happening outside my door, Dad walking around the flat filling black bin liners with the things he had decided belonged to him. When I came out to go to the loo he was back in his bedroom, filling more bags. I walked around the living room and saw the exposed spaces where ornaments had been, squares and circles in the dust, the empty rectangle on the mantelpiece where Candy's ashes had been. I peeked around the door into his room, the room that had once been Candy's, her red pencil scrawls still on the walls. The fabrics had been pulled from the ceiling, his Bedouin tent interior had been dismantled, was now just piles of dusty rugs and cushions and dead incense sticks. Dad was sitting on the carpet, his legs outstretched, body floppy, like a rag doll. He was wearing faded blue tracksuit bottoms and his Run the World T-shirt with the arms snipped off so it was more of a vest. He was still tanned from the holiday. He was crying, his body shaking with tears. I hated seeing him cry, a full-grown man. He used to sit on the sofa wearing Candy's pink coat, her ashes on his lap, crying.

I did not go to him, hug him, try to comfort him, I just watched him.

He saw me, his eyes bloodshot, his mouth tragic, snot everywhere.

'She was my best friend, G.'

And for a moment I didn't understand whom he was talking about. Candy? Julia? And then I realized he was talking about Mum.

SO WHY DID YOU FUCKING DO IT THEN? I wanted to shout. But I did not.

Dad's new flat wasn't totally like home, though; there were interesting differences. There was a nasty blue velour sofa and on the windowsill was a window box overflowing with tiny blue, yellow and pink flowers which tumbled and glistened with the water that he was now spraying with a water gun.

I had never known him grow anything.

'Those are nice,' I said, although I didn't mean it.

'I know. Aren't they great? The first thing I did when I moved in was to get myself down to the garden centre.'

He sprayed a plume of water in my direction. I did not smile.

He'd only been here four weeks and already he seemed so relaxed, so at home, so fucking happy. I stood in the centre of the room not knowing whether to sit or to go to where he was. What I really wanted to do was look around the flat, investigate every inch of it, work out in what ways he had made it similar to our home and in what ways it was different. But I didn't do that, because it would have seemed like a compliment and I didn't want him to think I admired his place, or what he had done, in any way.

'Sit down. I'll get you a drink.'

I lowered myself into the sofa. It was deep and the springs had gone, so my bottom sunk lower than my knees in a way I did not find comfortable or relaxing and it took some effort to remain rigidly upright. I heard a fridge opening, glasses clinking. I heard him humming. I stood up, took the chance to have a closer look about. He must have tidied very recently, I thought. There was no grime on any of the surfaces; the carpet had been hoovered. Was this how he had always wanted to live, or had he just made an effort because I was coming round?

He walked back into the room dangling two glasses upside down and holding an opened bottle of wine. He was wearing jeans that had been ironed, socks, a clean shirt, a belt. He looked smart. He put the glasses on a wooden coffee table and poured the wine. It was white. I went back to sit on the sofa.

'It's all right, here, isn't it?' he said, sounding nonchalant, even though it was such a big question.

I drank the wine, looked around; the evening sun was casting a soft, orange glow over everything, the light hazy and indulgent.

'Yeah,' I said and I took a cigarette from the packet on the table, lit it, inhaled deeply. I felt a bit better for that. He lit a joint that had been waiting, ready-rolled, in the ashtray.

He used to blow the smoke from his joint into my face to stop me crying and put a tot of whisky in my bottle to help me sleep.

'I've been thinking, imagine if you hadn't blown dope smoke in my face when I was a baby, imagine that. I'd be so clever, with all those extra brain cells, I'd be like Stephen Hawking.'

He looked at me, his cheeks ballooned; then he opened his lips and blew a thick plume of smoke in my direction.

'Why would you want to be in a fucking wheelchair?'

He laughed at his joke. But I was being serious. Imagine what I would have been like if you weren't my dad. The life I would have. The person I would be. None of this bullshit.

He swallowed his laughter when he realized that I was not joining in.

'How are the girls?' he asked.

'Fine,' I replied.

'And how's your mum?'

'She's well,' I said. 'She's started doing dancing classes.'

I didn't tell him about how much weight she'd lost, or her new plan to do an access course so that she could finally go to university, or the Italian man with a big moustache whom she'd had a couple of dinners with. I didn't want Dad to just make a joke out of it all, the way he always did.

'Bloody hell. Not ballet, I hope?'

'No, not ballet.'

There was silence between us. I listened to the familiar crackle of the Rizla paper as his joint burned down. I listened to the birdsong coming in through the window, which he had opened as wide as possible. He offered me the soggy joint. He had already smoked nearly half of it. I shook my head. He took another drag, holding his mouth shut, not breathing for as long as he could stand it, then coughing out the smoke and leaving the joint in the ashtray.

'Let's go out. My treat,' he said, his voice croaky.

It was better almost as soon as we left the flat. It felt good to be outside, with him, walking to a restaurant, a thing we had done together so many times. I began to talk, about how Mum was going to get a lodger, about how Anya had a new boyfriend and he was a DJ at the Fridge nightclub in Brixton. Dad laughed and smoked and when we walked through the door of the Indian restaurant they greeted him like a regular. The waiters all knew him by name, knew where he liked to sit, what he liked to drink, what he liked to eat. When the manager came by to say hello he looked at me for a moment in confusion.

'This is my daughter,' Dad said quickly.

'Hi,' I said.

How many times had he brought her here, what did people think, did they think she was his daughter, how did he explain it?

I ate popadoms and the spinach and lamb curry I always had at Indian restaurants. I let Dad steal a bit because he liked it too, we had some beers, and the simple acts of eating, drinking and smoking made me feel happy, and not just in a superficial, in-the-moment kind of way, but the pleasure I found in these things gave me a deeper sort of contentment, because I understood that it did not take much to make me happy, even when life was awful, and that was a relief.

'How's school? You working hard?'

I laughed. It was amazing that he still thought he had the right to ask me questions like that.

'Fuck off,' I said.

'Come on. You're so bright, you don't want to throw it away. You don't want to end up like me. I never passed an exam in my life.'

Dyslexic, left-handed, blew up the science block, left school at fourteen, virtually illiterate. I was never going to end up like him.

'Yes, I am working hard,' I said.

'Good girl.'

He waved his hand in the air, making a little signing motion to get the bill. He got me to sign the credit card slip for him because I had been copying his signature for years, and this was a fun thing that we had always done. We walked back to the flat. He told me he was planning to get a moped because the commute from Putney to Knightsbridge was such a nightmare. He pointed out the pub and the corner shop and the leisure centre. He said he had started swimming. I had never known him to do any exercise before.

It was night by the time we got back to the flat.

'You can stay over whenever you want,' he was saying as we walked back up the stairs. 'I could make you a great little bed on the floor in the sitting room. I tried it out last night, with the sofa cushions and a few pillows and stuff.'

'OK,' I said, wondering if I ever would stay here. I had missed him at home, especially when it was late and my thoughts turned dark. It seemed weird and sad that he wasn't in the flat, where he had always been, just a door away. His absence made the shape of the place feel different, so that it didn't feel like where I had grown up, so that it didn't feel like home.

He opened the door and I followed him in. But would this place ever feel like home? Could it? It had just as much right to; Dad was here, as were so many of the familiar things from my childhood. Could I run away here if I needed to, even though there was no space for me, even though I would have to sleep on two sofa cushions on the floor?

Dad kicked off his Converse trainers. 'I'm going for a crap,' he said.

I waited until he had shut the door to the loo before I went into his bedroom.

It was dark in there; the curtains were pulled across, so not even the bright moonlight could get through. I stood near the entrance to the room, not sure how much further I wanted to go. It smelt of him, like his bedroom had always smelt, of sweat and sleep, but there was something new, and that was sex.

A large picture was propped up on the chest of drawers. There was enough light coming in from the hall that I could just about make it out. At first I thought it was an Indian thing, a postcard of a mythical female; Dad liked little statues of Ganesh and laughing fat-bellied Buddhas. But this was too weird for that, the creature's upper body was white and where its legs should have been there was a black, tangled confusion, as though it was half-woman, half-octopus.

It took seconds for me to have these thoughts, for me to work out what I was looking at.

It was her.

It was Julia. Idiot. Of course that's who it was. In bed. The blackness was the duvet; underneath were her human legs, not tentacles. Dad had taken this photograph before they'd had sex? After they'd had sex? Then, days later, he'd gone to the shop to get the picture developed, blown up.

I moved closer to the photo, to see it better, even though it made me feel sick, lamb and spinach curry travelling back up my throat. Julia had something around her waist. It was a gold chain, his gold chain, the one he had worn around his neck all my life, the one with Candy's bite marks in it, so much a part of him, like his hair or his eyes, so much a part of us. And it was around her waist.

I heard the loo flush. I stepped out of the bedroom and into the hall.

He opened the door. He was not wearing his chain, it was not around his neck, which meant that she had it, wherever she was right now, the soft gold against her pink skin. He was hers and she was his. That was it. I didn't belong here.

'I've got to go,' I said.

'What are you talking about? I thought you were going to stay the night.'

'No,' I said.

'Let me call you a cab, at least.'

'No.'

No, no, no.

I ran down the steps and out of the door so I wouldn't have time to change my mind. It had suddenly got cold outside and the shock of this made me breathe again, a big gulp of air, as if I had been drowning. I started walking, away from that building, from him, from that photograph. I only stopped when I got to the end of the street and turned the corner. I knew Dad. I knew what he would do. He would stand there for a moment, shocked, angry, upset. Then he would remember what he ought to do, as a father, so he would grab his keys, stumble down the stairs, hoping to find me still there. He would open the front door, imagining that I would be outside on the doorstep and it would be easy and he would only have to say, 'Come back up.' And I would reply, 'Oh, all right then.'

When he did not find me outside he would stand

there for a while, he would look down the street, he might even call for me. 'G!'

But he would go no further.

'She could be anywhere by now,' he would tell himself. 'There's nothing else I can do.'

He would shake his head and feel a bit bad but console himself with the thought that he had done all he could. Under the circumstances.

I knew, by then, how far he would go for me.

25

2015, London

Who am I?

I am a younger sister, older sister, middle child, only child.

I am the daughter of a junkie hairdresser and an alcoholic model, daughter of a sex-addict drug dealer and a born-again Christian accountant. Before my sister died I was the good one, the sensible one, more like Mum than Dad, hiding behind my pink-rimmed NHS glasses, hand up in class with the answer to every question ('Give the other children a chance, Gavanndra'). But after Candy died I had to be her as well as me. I absorbed her, split myself in half (shattered into a million pieces). I became the naughty girl, the wild girl, Daddy's girl.

I am a bereaved sister, bereaved daughter, bad sister, bad daughter. I am a mother, wife, friend. Keeper of memories, teller of stories. Greedy and funny. Cold and intimidating. Loyal and loving. Survivor (how I hate that word).

I never wanted anyone to feel sorry for me because that would mean that they saw someone who was broken. I don't want to be broken. I don't want to feel sorry for myself. I have no patience with people who indulge in self-pity. Get up and fix yourself. Why are you waiting for someone else to do it for you? Who do you think is going to save you? There is only you. There is only me.

Alone.

Angry.

When I go to see Fiona we don't talk about Candy, we don't talk about Dad, we don't talk about Mum, we talk about me. Fiona asks me to imagine the younger version of myself, the child who had to make her own breakfast, whose parents were too high to remember significant acts like conception.

'Imagine she is sitting opposite you. Give her a name.'

I call her Newt after the little girl in the second *Alien* film, who lives alone on a spaceship and has seen her parents devoured by a terrifying alien with glutinous saliva dripping from its many pin-sharp teeth.

'How do you feel about her?'

Maternal. I want to give her a bath, give her dinner, put her to bed in clean sheets, read her stories, hug her till she falls asleep, be right there by her side if she wakes in the night. Make her feel safe.

'Yes, that is what I want to do too,' says Fiona.

And it feels good. Imagining it makes it feel as if it has actually happened. Newt's grubby face is clean now; her hair is brushed; she's had second helpings of roast chicken.

'Now think about fifteen-year-old you. Imagine her sitting opposite you.'

Drunk, high, smoking, laddered tights, black around the eyes, greasy hair. Bitch, liar, cheat. She makes my stomach flip in revulsion. I don't want to be in the same room as her, let alone be her.

'I can't.'

'Why not?'

'She's horrible.'

'But don't you want to hug her, clean her face, make her feel safe? Don't you want to look after her?'

'No,' I say, becoming bolshy and uncommunicative, staring Fiona down. 'No.'

Fifteen-year-old me is not sitting over there any more, she has moved inside me, her painful energy filling my veins. I am becoming her again. I want to rip her out of me.

'But I do. I want to hug her just as much as I want to hug Newt,' says Fiona, making a hugging motion.

'I can't stand her. I am so ashamed of her,' I say, and I drop my head.

'I don't see why. She was pretty amazing. Think of all she lived through, think of what she achieved, think of the good choices she made.'

I come home and look at the diaries I wrote when I was fourteen, fifteen, sixteen, hoping to find someone in there that I can love as much as Fiona seems to (perhaps she is the mad one!).

The diaries are scrawling and incoherent, all about getting pissed, getting high, going out, dressing up. Occasionally there are a few lines of Latin vocab, a burst of coherence in the chaos, but mostly it is furious black ink, swearing and showing off. Incidents are written down, Julia, Adrian, Dad, nightclubs, restaurants and raves, but never how these people or places made me feel. Neither of my sisters, Candy or Maranda, are really mentioned.

Is this it, the extent of my innermost thoughts? Is this a depiction of my sixteen-year-old soul? No wonder I hate who I was.

I have lunch with someone I knew from school whom I have recently got in touch with again. Kate sat next to me in Latin for two years during our GCSEs, and in front of me during the exam.

'I just remember you writing and writing, pages of it. I remember asking you, "What do you do with it, all the words?" and you said, "I burn them. I burn everything."'

I do not remember the burning or the writing. What was I writing? Why was I burning it? Is it because I found it all so horrible that even though I knew I had to get the words out of me, words that felt like fire in my chest, I couldn't let those words exist in the world?

I can't stop thinking about what Kate told me. It feels like an act of kindness, to have kept this memory of mine safe all these years, to give it back to me when I was able to hold it once more. And it is not just an act of kindness to the person I am now, it is an act of kindness to the girl I was then.

There were other acts of kindness. Not everyone disliked me as much as I disliked myself.

My teachers agreed that even though I had not achieved the grades that I should have I could still take the A-levels

I had chosen. Latin, Chemistry and Ancient History. I was given a huge second chance. So I took it. I studied. I plunged myself into Virgil, Herodotus, protons, electrons, carbon bonds, Athenian democracy and the Roman Republic. At night I dreamt of dusty hoplites with long spears and Persians with golden armour and hair slickly curled. By the time I was seventeen I was doing well enough for my teachers to suggest Cambridge University. My Latin teacher, Miss Yeats, had watched my transformation from a studious Tolkein-loving twelve-year-old still trying to get her head around the move from a state school to a private school, so much catching up to do (I had never done French or played tennis), to a smoking, back-chatting fifteen-year-old who was rarely at school and who, when she was, was hungover or high. It was Miss Yeats who arranged for me to go to Newnham College for a meeting with the director of studies for Classics, Professor Mary Beard. Miss Yeats wanted me to see what a different life might look like, and whether I might want that life for myself.

I wore a long floral skirt, a purple mohair jumper and glasses. I dressed up as the girl I wanted to be. Serious and studious. I sat outside Mary's office, the interiors quiet and ornate, a white curling balustrade and dark wooden cabinets. I remembered how I used to steal the black Penguin classics from the Classics room at school, translations of Euripides and Sophocles, Aristotle and Lucretius. I had a whole bookshelf full of them. I didn't read them, but I did dust them, made sure they looked neat, tightly packed, spines shiny with care. My bookshelf was a sacred place; the rest of my bedroom was a grubby mess: dirty pants, teacups floating with green mould and orange peel that had been used as an ashtray.

In Mary's room – high-ceilinged, long-windowed, looking out on to the green of the vast gardens – the books were part of the mess. There were so many piles of them, higgledy-piggledy, just one more pamphlet or journal would send them tumbling like a domino run.

I didn't want to end up as a waitress on the King's Road, sitting on men's laps to get drinks bought for me, laughing at jokes that weren't funny, selling a bit of coke to my friends on the side. I wanted this.

So I worked harder than ever. I got my A-level results, got my place at Newnham. I remember the day the letter arrived from Cambridge, a January morning. I opened it with shivering fingers.

I cut my hair, bought sensible black leather loafers, took out most of the gold hoops from my self-pierced ears. I went to live in Rome for six months so I could practise being this new person, a girl who loved Latin literature, Roman history, Kate Bush and Russian novels. In Rome I didn't have to tell people about my dad or my sister, all the shitty things that I had done. In Rome I learnt that it was so much easier to be me when I was pretending to be someone else.

26

1994, Rome

'My father is coming to visit.'

It was more a spoken thought than a conversational offering. We'd talked on the phone that day and Dad had asked me to arrange a hotel for him and Julia. He'd already gone to the travel agent's and bought cheap flights. He would be here next weekend. It was something he'd talked about doing before I left. I hadn't realized he'd been planning to bring Julia too.

'That's great!' said Giuseppe.

We were sitting on the pink sateen bedcover on the bed in my room. We were watching television. This was the only television in the flat and often we would all gather in my room in the evenings, lounging, smoking. But it was late and everyone else had gone to bed so it was just me and Giuseppe. He didn't even live here; he was a friend of one of my flatmates.

He laughed. On telly three men in shirts with the top buttons undone, displaying impressively hairy chests, were gesticulating with their cigarettes, interrupting each other and shouting. It was a programme about politics and I couldn't really follow it. I preferred *Rimini*

Jazz!, an entertainment show with performers singing jaunty ballads against a backdrop of the sea at sunset.

'This guy, he is so funny, he is comedian, but he know everything about politics, he is so funny,' said Giuseppe.

Giuseppe was wearing a white T-shirt and jeans. He had taken his shoes off, but was still wearing his grey socks. He was tall, over six feet I reckoned, with blond hair, long on top, short at the sides, and blue eyes. He was a law student from Bari. His favourite film was *Unforgiven* with Clint Eastwood and he didn't speak very good English, but his blue eyes were fringed with long black lashes and he had an amazing smile, wide and wild. He looked more like a Viking than a Roman.

I felt the side of my body that was closest to him tingle with the electricity of anticipation.

'What he is, your father?'

'Do you mean what does he do?'

'*Sì*. Sorry. Yes.'

I had told Giuseppe that I would help him with his English. He was meant to be helping me with my Italian too, but so far that had just involved watching lots of television together.

'My dad runs his own business,' I said, thinking that is not a lie.

'That is good,' he said.

Giuseppe's father was important in the army, something to do with fighter jets; his friends called his father 'Il Generale', which made him sound intimidating. I wondered if Giuseppe's father and my father would ever meet. On our wedding day perhaps. But not before that, not before it was really necessary.

'He's got shops,' I said. This was also not a lie. We did call the salon 'the shop'. And once there had been shops plural, in Covent Garden, in Soho, even in Camden, when things were going well, when he was sober.

'Great,' said Giuseppe, and he coughed and shifted a tiny bit closer to me. I realized that he was nervous, and that made me light up inside, because it meant he might actually like me.

The programme finished.

'Do you want to come to the Forum with me tomorrow?' I asked.

'Il Foro? *Certo!* Yes. I've never been. Can you believe?'

'Great, shall we meet at eleven?'

'OK. Good. I go now.'

He kissed me chastely on either cheek. I felt the warmth of his skin, his rough stubble, concentrating hard so I would never forget that feeling, him touching me, his hand on my shoulder. I was too scared, too self-conscious, to turn my head so that our lips might meet, which is what I wanted to do. More than anything.

He slid his feet into his brown loafers, put on his coat and picked up his motorcycle helmet.

'*Domani!*' he said, raising a palm in farewell.

The next day I wore tights, a black skirt, black loafers, a blue T-shirt and a denim jacket. I brushed my hair and put on a little bit of make-up. I was a Classics student on my year off between school and university, absorbing

198

the sights and smells of Rome, trying to find ancient history in a modern city. That is what I was and that is what I wanted to look like. It was spring in Rome but the sky was grey. Giuseppe was dashing in a long black coat. He paid for us both to get in and he bought me the guidebook.

We walked together among the inexplicable broken stones, under swaying pillars, beneath triumphal arches. Giuseppe was gentlemanly; if ever the path was too narrow for us to walk side by side he would gesture that I should go first. I explained things to him: this is where Julius Caesar was assassinated, this is where Mark Anthony made his speech, this is where the Vestal Virgins lived, this is where they kept the grain that fed the population of the city. There were nests of snarling kittens, overfull bins, groups of bored schoolchildren, but I saw none of that, I only saw the magic of the place, stepping where the Romans had once walked, the space between then and now not so wide, not really, if I was here and they had once been here too.

'Will you bring your father here too? You are a very good guide,' said Giuseppe.

'Maybe,' I said.

I wasn't sure I wanted to alter my memory of this place by coming here with Dad and Julia. I wasn't sure how I felt about Dad coming at all. The skies were so wide here and I was so free. I was unfurling in the sunlight. I didn't want him to come and squash everything, without even realizing he was doing anything wrong.

'Who, me? Don't be mean to your old dad.'

We went for pizza afterwards in Suburra, the slum where Caesar was raised. We talked about film, music, food. The language barrier made it hard for us to talk about much more. We did not talk about my life before I'd come here, carrying a suitcase filled with dictionaries, primers and Latin texts, so heavy I could barely lift it.

Dad and Julia's flight landed at 11 p.m. We'd agreed that they would get a cab directly to the hotel and I would pick them up the next morning. They were only here for two days and Dad had never been to Italy before. I wanted to show him as much as possible. I thought that in the morning we could go to the Porta Portese flea market, then lunch in Trastevere and then we could go up to the Capitoline Museums – we could see the bronze of Romulus and Remus suckling the wolf and the statue of Laocoön and his sons being squeezed to death by the two serpents sent by Athena. That would be fun. Then they would probably want to stop and have a drink somewhere.

I arrived at the hotel at 11 a.m., as planned. The hotel was actually on the eighth floor of a building. I had to go up in an old-fashioned lift that shuddered and whined as it ascended.

Julia had left school and was now working as a receptionist in Dad's salon.

I had not seen either Julia or my father for three months.

I asked the receptionist which room they were in. Away

from the reception area the hotel was shabbier than I had expected, a brown tiled floor with dust in the corners, thin wood-veneer doors, a pile of dirty bedsheets, the sound of two women arguing.

I knocked on their door. No answer. I knocked again. Perhaps they had already gone out, but they should have left a note at the very least.

Then I heard shuffling, grunting. Dad.

He opened the door, holding it and peering around it, eyes crusted with sleep. He rubbed the hair on his head, his arm hooked upwards, like a monkey.

It was as though I'd seen him only yesterday.

'Chubbs! What are you doing here?'

'It's eleven. We're meant to be going out.'

They weren't even ready. I couldn't believe it. Didn't they want to see the city?

'What are you talking about? No it's not.'

He staggered back to the bed, naked. It was not a big room; the bed took up most of it, a mess of white sheets and pillows with Julia at the centre. The place smelt of Paris perfume and Baileys liquor. They must have had fun in duty free.

'Shut the door, I ain't got any clothes on!'

'Who is it?' wailed Julia.

'Our leader.'

'What?'

'Gav Two.'

'Oh.'

'Do you want me to wait outside while you get dressed?'

'Don't worry about that, sit down!'

Dad pulled on a pair of boxer shorts and a T-shirt. I moved the torn-open pack of two hundred Silk Cut on to the floor so I could sit on the leather armchair that was shoved in the corner of the room.

'How was your flight?' I asked.

'It was great, wasn't it, J?' he said, addressing Julia.

'What's the time?' she said.

'Eleven,' I replied, checking my watch. 'Actually eleven seventeen.'

'Well, my watch says ten fifteen,' said Dad.

'It's the time difference. You didn't adjust your watches?' I said.

'There you go, I was right,' said Dad.

Julia groaned and pulled the sheets over her head.

'We really should get going,' I said. 'Otherwise . . .'

I wished he could have come by himself. I wished I could have shown him the place that I had learnt to love so much, just the two of us. It was impossible with her here.

'Come on, out of your pit, our leader has spoken!' said Dad, tugging the sheets off Julia.

My heart twisted in a way that I had forgotten about, that I had forgotten to prepare myself for. I had gone soft so fast.

'Gav!' she shouted, pulling the sheet back. She had black make-up smudged all around her eyes and had dyed her hair black too. She wrapped the sheet around her and got out of bed, trailing it behind her as she went into the bathroom, locking it. I heard her turn on the shower and her echoey squeal. 'It's cold!'

I smiled for the first time that day.

'So how have you been, Chubbs? We've missed you.'

'Really good, thanks.'

'Got a boyfriend yet?'

I blushed. I couldn't help it. 'No,' I said.

'You have, I can tell! Ha! J! She's got a boyfriend,' he shouted through the door as he pulled on his jeans. 'So what's his name?'

'I haven't got a boyfriend!'

'I hope he's better than that last one.'

I gave up saying I didn't have a boyfriend and smoked a cigarette instead. Julia was still showering. I checked my watch. It was now eleven thirty-nine.

'We really need to get going if we are not going to miss everything.'

'Chill out, girl! It's not going to disappear in a poof of smoke if we don't keep to the timetable.'

Julia came out of the shower, a towel wrapped around her body and another turbaned around her head.

'The towels are so thin in this place,' she said. Dad watched her admiringly. She went back into the bathroom and locked the door once again.

'How are you?' I asked.

'Really good. The shop's busy; I'm making a few bob. How are you doing for money?'

'Oh, OK. You know. I saved up quite a bit, but it goes fast. And my wallet got stolen out of my bag the first week I was here. It had quite a lot of cash in it, so that was annoying.'

Dad found his wallet among the ephemera on the

dressing table, lighters and asthma inhalers, make-up and magazines. He pulled out four fifty-pound notes. 'Here you go, my darling.'

'Thanks, Dad,' I said, taking the money and putting it in the little compartment inside my brown suede bag.

Dad took a white packet out of his wallet. 'Fancy a toot?' he said, waving it in my direction.

'No, thanks,' I replied, and sighed inside as I watched him mash the white powder and cut it into two lines with his debit card.

I took off my coat.

Fifteen minutes later Julia came out of the bathroom. She was wearing a pair of very tight black jeans, high heels with strappy bits around the ankle and a tiny purple Lycra wrap-around top. Her stomach was completely exposed. It was basically a bikini with arms.

'Is that what you're wearing?' I said. I couldn't help it – the words fell out of my mouth before I could stop them.

'Yeah,' she said, looking at me. Her hair was still wet, making damp patches on her top.

'I mean, it's just the shoes. We're going to be walking quite a bit, seeing quite a lot. I worry that your feet will start to hurt.'

'Oh, G, let's not do too much walking,' said Dad. 'We can get cabs, can't we? I'll pay. We are on holiday, remember.'

Julia had brought a hairdryer with her, but not an

adaptor plug. I went to reception to ask for one and when I came back they were giggling about something but went very quiet as soon as they saw me.

It was nearly twelve.

Julia spent a long time blow-drying her hair.

'Right, can we go now? I wanted us to pop into the flea market before we went for lunch.'

'Oh, I love flea markets!' said Julia, picking up her massive black make-up bag before going back into the bathroom and locking the door.

'Dad, we're not going to have time to see anything at this rate!'

'Give us a break. It's not our fault the clock's gone forward!'

Dad combed his hair and sprayed himself with so much Eau Sauvage aftershave that my nostrils stung.

'So where are we going for lunch then? I'm starving. We haven't had any breakfast.'

'I thought we could go over to Trastevere. It's really cool over there.'

'Can't we go for lunch next to that big fountain with the horses, the one in the film? That would be nice.'

'The Trevi Fountain? But the restaurants round there will cost a bomb, and the food won't even be that good – they will be filled with tourists.'

We left the hotel forty-five minutes later. Julia linked arms with Dad and I led them to the Trevi Fountain. Every man who passed us looked at Julia, whistled, said, '*Che bella!*' She was delighted. So was Dad.

We got a table in a restaurant in a little alleyway just

along from the Trevi Fountain, the menu translated into German, English and Japanese.

'This is perfect, G, isn't it perfect?'

'Yeah!' said Julia, who had already been given a red rose, for free, by the man trying to sell flowers to the tourists. After we'd finished lunch Dad ordered another bottle of wine.

'Let's just sit here for a bit, chill out, this is wonderful,' he said, and he passed his wallet to Julia, who went inside the restaurant to go to the loo and returned licking her lips and talking too fast.

We never did go to the museums, or the Bocca della Verità, or the Vatican, or any of the other places I had planned. They loved the flea market though, where the stall holders stared at Julia, open-mouthed, and she bought a little Virgin Mary icon.

'How was your father's trip to Roma?' asked Giuseppe.

'Great, thanks. We did loads of stuff. Saw the Pantheon, the Trevi Fountain, all the museums. My feet are killing me, we did so much walking.'

'Poor feet,' he said.

We were sitting next to each other on my bed. Everyone else had gone to sleep. The closing credits to *Rimini Jazz!* were playing.

'You want I can massage your feet?'

'That would be lovely.'

I turned off the television and the room went dark. I pulled myself up on to the bed, stretched out my legs, my feet bare. Giuseppe took my foot. He massaged the sole with one hand and stroked my leg with the other. The room was very quiet. Outside the sirens wailed and the Vespas revved. Giuseppe finished with my feet and shuffled further up the bed. He pushed my hair from my forehead. Leant forwards, his face coming towards mine.

My heart untwisted.

I knew that his father would never meet my father, but that didn't matter, not at all.

27

2015, London

How can I tell people who I am?

I have spent over two decades pretending to be a different person, someone who fits in with the world that I find myself a part of. When people meet me they make so many easy assumptions: nice family, good school, fancy university, impressive job. Some people still ask questions though: why have you got such a funny name, do you have any brothers or sisters, where do you come from? And I never know what to say, where to start or where to stop. I can't just tell them about the girls and Dad, because I would have to explain about Candy too. I can't just talk about Dad selling cocaine to pay his half of my school fees – I have to talk about the heroin and the junkies in the sitting room. I can't just talk about one death – I have to talk about two. It's all connected: tug on one memory and I find half a dozen more jangling behind it.

So usually, unless I am feeling particularly antagonistic (at an awards dinner sitting next to the male editor of a magazine, so self-important and patronizing, who looks at me as if to say I know what you are, so I use my story as a weapon) I'll either swerve the conversation or offer the PG version: London childhood, hippic parents, a bit wild . . .

Whom am I protecting?

At school everyone knew everything about me and it made me feel like a freak show. I couldn't wait to leave, to escape to a different city, to start the remaking of myself, to be in charge of my own story. And along the way I learnt how to shed people. I have hardly any friends from my childhood, people who knew too much, who looked at me and saw death, drugs, that savage self-confidence which comes from desperation.

But that is not what Fiona sees, even when she looks at the teenaged version of me.

Maybe I am not the things that happened to me.

I decide to start telling the truth. I start gently. I tell someone I have known for over fifteen years, a good friend, about Candy.

'But, Gav, I never knew,' she says, crying over red wine and steak in a restaurant in Paris.

I make a decision that from now on, if someone asks, if someone really seems to want to know, then I will tell them everything. Sometimes this is tough when you have only just met and it is a nice dinner party with lovely food and fancy wine, because it is too much. Sometimes they turn their head away looking shell-shocked and I think, I shouldn't have spoken.

But then they have a sip of wine and turn back to face me and suddenly we are no longer talking about the mundane things, like holidays or schools, we are talking about the Big Things, death and betrayal and loss and chaos.

And the more I do it, the more I talk to people, old friends and new ones, the more I discover that we are all hiding some sort of darkness, that the PG version is only ever half the story and the other half is always much more important.

After these conversations I don't feel like a freak show any more, I feel lucky to still be here, lucky to have such good friends. Things have changed, me and the people around me.

I take it a step further. I decide to write an article about what happened to Candy, what happened to me, about how we suppress grief when it is too hard to face, what that suppression does to us. If Candy's story is told in a magazine, if her photograph is printed, if that story is put online and people share it, that will blow life back into her memory.

Kate, the editor of *Tatler*, is coming back from maternity leave, which means I don't have to be in charge any more and will have the time to do this. Once I start writing I find that the words come fast; they were in me, just waiting to come out, impatient. *Why have you waited so long?*

Kate is the first person to read the article, then the sub-editors and the picture editors. Everyone sends kind messages and many people cry. I am pleased at their tears because those are tears for Candy. After the piece is published people I have never met get in touch to tell me how much the piece moved them and helped them, how they lost a sister, a brother, a parent and have never properly grieved, but now they will.

The article upsets my mother too, but not in the way I expected.

'I didn't realize that you haven't got any memories of Candy,' she says.

It is as if she is offended that I have not told her this, as if keeping this from her is another example of our lack of intimacy, another betrayal; I would have told my father.

'I'm sorry,' I say.

'Do you want to talk about it? You could come over; we could go through the albums. I could tell you about her?'

This was something Fiona had suggested. 'Talk to your mother about Candy,' she said. 'Cry with her, console each other.'

But I can't do it. I can talk to everyone else in the world about Candy. But not my mother. That still feels too hard.

'No, Mum, I don't think I want to do that just yet. Maybe one day.'

28

1997, Cambridge and London

It was the quiet I loved the most.

Or was it the smell of cut grass?

I couldn't decide.

I hadn't known, before I came here, that I actually preferred silence to noise, green spaces to grey ones, early mornings to late nights. It took me a whole year to settle, to stop going back down to London every weekend, to realize that this was where I wanted to be. In my room, in my college, with my books, photocopies of Greek bronzes and Roman busts Blu-Tacked to the walls.

My dictionaries and stationery were arranged neatly on the desk that faced the gardens. My Latin dictionary bulged awkwardly. I reached instead for my Ancient Greek dictionary, for my guide to irregular Greek verbs, my copy of *Agamemnon*, its translation, my lined notepad. I ran my index finger along the lines of poetry, trying to get a sense of what I was reading, puzzling my way into that slow trance state. When I got to a word I didn't know I would look it up in the dictionary and then write it down in neat biro. I squared off verbs in sharpened pencil, underlined matching nouns and adjectives, checked the commentary frequently, wrote prompts alongside the text. I was not the sort to turn up to class with a Loeb (those little red or green hardback books with the text on one side and the English on the other) and pretend to translate. Everyone knew you were doing it anyway, the sham pauses, the reaching for words: 'Dagger, no sword, he raised his sword . . .', the rush towards translation. Everyone knew, especially the professors; they'd been watching students do it for decades.

What was the point in being here if you were going to pretend? That was what I thought. I'd fought too hard to get here for that. And I loved the past, its grammar and its drama. Virgil made me feel safe; Julius Caesar made me feel excited.

The Oresteia was tough though, doom intoned from 2,500 years ago with syntax that was fluid and mysterious. The short lines of poetry were spidery and marked with inexplicable lines and dots. Things got easier with Euripides.

After seventeen lines I put two slices of brown bread in the toaster. I continued to translate, brushing crumbs from my notepad as I drank tea. I stopped once I got to thirty-five lines. It didn't look like much but it had taken me nearly an hour.

I got dressed, putting on a short black corduroy skirt, a tight blue T-shirt and black wedge mules. I brushed my hair and put on some mascara. I put my key in my pocket and let the door slam behind me, carrying my text and vocabulary list.

I walked along the parquet corridors, past communal kitchens that smelt of Chinese five-spice, pushing through double doors that swung behind me as I walked, like ripples in the sea.

Professor Pat Easterling's rooms were in one of the newer parts of the building, a square annexe with low ceilings and better toilets. Prof Pat, we called her. The other girls in my year, Elaine, Holly and Kiran, were already waiting, their skirts elasticated and their shoes earnest.

'Hi,' I said. 'That was a tough bit of prep!'

'Oh yes,' said Holly.

'I spent all yesterday evening doing it,' said Elaine.

Holly checked her watch. 'It's time,' she said. She approached the door and knocked three times.

'Come in!' said the voice from the other side.

Holly opened the door and we followed her in.

'Hello, ladies!' said Prof Pat, who mostly wore muted purple tweeds, even in June, and light-responsive spectacles, so that on sunny days it looked as though she was wearing sunglasses. She was sitting in a low armchair with her back to her patio doors, which opened out on to the gardens, with their bright lawns and lavish herbaceous borders, tended by a large team of gardeners.

'Sorry, sorry, we're late,' said Emma, rushing in with Becca, both holding their Loebs, trailing long, unbrushed hair, their clothes jangling with bells and twinkling with mirrors.

'Not to worry, sit down,' said Prof Pat. Books were piled on the desk behind her and arranged on the shelves, including a number of copies of her edition of *The Trachiniae*. 'As it is our last session I thought we might have a little sherry to celebrate. A whole term of nine a.m. Aeschylus. Bravo!'

Small and delicately etched glasses had already been arranged on a tray. Prof Pat poured a little sherry into each glass and handed them around.

'Not for me, thanks,' said Elaine.

'I'll have hers,' said Emma.

Prof Pat smiled and sat down. 'Let's begin.'

I sipped the sherry. It reminded me of my Dad's parents in Bromley, of my grandparents' living room with the turquoise settee and the china figurines of gay ladies with china baskets and china poodles, of the story Dad loved to tell about Mum when she was still drinking. She had got pissed at lunch and had gone up to Grandma and Grandpa's bedroom to go through Dad's jacket pockets, hoping to find a bit of coke to freshen her up. She found a little paper packet containing powder, and racked herself up a line on the glass-topped dressing table, did it, and then boom, her head exploded, blood trickled from her nose, and she fell off the pink pastel-coloured velour pouffe, tumbling to the deeply carpeted floor with a thud that had Dad, Grandma, Grandpa, me and even the aggressive Pekingese, Tinker, running up the stairs. What Mum had thought was cocaine was actually heroin, but unlike Uma Thurman in *Pulp Fiction*, Mum did not need an injection of adrenaline to her heart to bring her round, Dad just slapped her cheeks a bit and got her to drink a sugary cup of tea. She couldn't make it up the steep lawn to the car, though; she had to crawl on her hands and knees.

He falls, convulses, his soul rushes out,
A gush of murder-blood spouts from him,
Spattering me with a shower of dark red dew,
Like the rain Zeus sends down to make
    the crops bud,
And I rejoice.

Clytemnestra has just slit the throat of her husband Agamemnon in revenge for his sacrifice of their daughter.

'Lovely translation, thank you,' said Prof Pat.

I took the long way back to my room, through the gardens, brushing my hands through the warm lavender, catching a jasmine bloom and rubbing it between my finger and thumb so I would still be able to smell it hours later. I loved to spend whole afternoons lying on the grass, reading, translating, sleeping, the dense and expertly tended lawn soft like a thick carpet.

I walked up the steps to the entrance of my part of the college building. I just had to drop off my books and get the things I needed for the trip to London.

I bumped into my friend Lorna on the other side of the door.

'I've been looking for you! I've just been to your room. But you weren't there.'

'That's because I am here,' I said. I felt a little tipsy from the sherry, from the poetry, from the scented gardens.

'I was just wondering if you could sort me out too. You know.'

Lorna looked at me, her straight eyebrows rising towards the middle of her forehead, creating a triangular effect, a Hellenistic facial expression, tragic and mournful.

'Lorn, I'm really sorry, but it's all been settled,' I said.

'I've got the money here. Please. Otherwise I will just be cadging off you all night.'

This was true. Lorna took two notes from the pocket of her jeans and handed them to me.

'OK. I'll see. I've got to go,' I said.

I felt sharper, less woozy and romantic, as I walked up the stairs to my room, Lorna's money folded into my palm. At the bottom of the next flight of stairs my friend Naomi sat on a step smoking and reading Wyndham Lewis, a little ceramic bowl next to her for the ash. She spent most of her time here because she was a chain-smoker who did not like to smoke in her own room.

'You're off now?' said Naomi.

'Yes,' I replied. 'I won't be long though.'

How was it that everyone knew about this trip?

I opened the door to my room. My mobile phone was upright in its charger. I normally just left it there, but decided it might be a good idea to take it today.

I opened my Latin dictionary and removed the enve-lope I had placed there for safekeeping, adding Lorna's forty pounds. I felt as if I was in a film as I did this, a film about spies, perhaps, or covert activities. I pushed the envelope to the bottom of my black Kookai bag, along with my phone, my wallet, some lip gloss and a book; although there would be no time for reading.

Dan was parked just outside the front gate. He wasn't

really allowed to be parked there. I walked across the cobbles fast, not wanting us to get into trouble.

'Hiya!' he said, smiling through the window.

I got in, stretched across to kiss his cheek hello. There was a half-smoked joint in the ashtray.

'Lorna wants me to get some for her too,' I said as we drove over the bridge, cyclists swarming on either side, grand college buildings looming ahead of us.

'So does Tom. Didn't he tell you?'

'No, he didn't. For fuck's sake,' I said.

I composed the text message as we drove past King's, St John's, forbidden lawns and old gates, past tourists and famous cake shops. *Hi, I'd like two more tickets for the show please, thanks. Gx.*

'We're going to get there on time, aren't we?' I said.

'Of course we are,' replied Dan.

I was happier once we were out of town and on to the motorway. I performed the same passenger duties for Dan that I would perform for my father, changing the music, lighting cigarettes, one for him, one for me, winding down the car window and singing along to whatever song was playing. It was hard to wind the window back up though; the glass kept slipping down, even as I was turning the handle. Dan's car was red and had been purchased from an old lady in his parents' village. Dan had crashed it, just the once, and it had been patched up by the village mechanic.

'It's basically stuck together with superglue,' he explained, which was why it rattled whenever he took the speed over forty miles per hour.

We were in the fast lane, doing ninety, ramming up behind slower cars so that they would move out of our way. We listened to the same song by Josh Wink three times, rewinding it again and again.

No problem x came the reply to my text.

We were meant to be meeting Neil at midday, and we were making good time, speeding away from professors and sherry, herbaceous borders and cobbled entrances; back to London, to gritty streets and dodgy deals.

The Raven wasn't busy. It wasn't the sort of place people came to for lunch, with its black-painted concrete floor and shabby seats. People came here at night. People like my dad, his friends Neil, Dodge and Del, petty criminals who ran gangs of teenagers on bikes out of the World's End estate, who sold drugs and stolen goods. Dad always got my Christmas present from Del, usually a stolen scented candle, but last year a man's Adidas shell suit because that was all he'd had left.

'But you said you wanted to get into running, G, I thought you'd like it!'

I wondered if Neil had told Dad that we were meeting like this.

Neil was sitting in the corner, a copy of the *Evening Standard* on the table in front of him, and a half-pint of lager which he had not yet drunk from.

'Hello, my darlin',' he said.

I had never got to the bottom of how Neil and Dad knew each other. He had been a club promoter, or in the music business, or something like that. Dad had helped him out with publicity once upon a time, or done the hair of one of his artistes. They went back a long way, that was all I knew for certain.

'Hi, Neil,' I said.

He was wearing a baggy leather jacket, the sleeves pushed up so the cuffs were tight around his elbows. He had a gold watch and tightly curled hair, black but grey-ing, almost squared off at the corners, as if it had been cut with hedge-trimmers.

'Fancy a drink?' he said, motioning at his half-pint.

I didn't want a drink. I still had the taste of sherry in my mouth and the smell of jasmine on my fingers. But I wondered if I ought to have a drink, for show.

'I'm fine, thanks, actually,' I said.

'How's uni?'

'Really good, thanks.'

I wondered why he called it uni, not university, why he was so familiar about a place he had never been.

'My son probably won't go to uni. I mean, he wants to be a motor-racing driver, so he doesn't see the point, but I say it's important to have something else up your sleeve.'

'I suppose. But there is no point doing it if you don't want to. It's a lot of hard work. And he's doing well with the driving, anyway, isn't he?'

'Oh yes, really well.'

We paused to eye each other meaningfully.

'So it's ten tickets,' I said, and I was surprised at the sound of my voice saying those words, and surprised by the tense feeling in my throat, by how aware I was that I was swallowing noisily and that my fingertips felt unusually warm.

He pushed the *Evening Standard* towards me.

'Have you read the newspaper today?' he said.

'No,' I replied.

'I think you should. I think you should take it away with you.'

'OK,' I said, and I laid my tingling palm on the paper, felt the ink adhere to my skin, and felt something lumpy, something that shouldn't be there, beneath the thin pages.

Neil stood up and walked around the table so that he was standing next to me. I twisted my body to look up at him. I realized then he was doing this on purpose, to shield the barman's view of me.

'Do you have something for me?' he said.

I reached down under the table to find my bag. There was a shaft of sunlight coming through the window, illuminating the dinginess of the pub interior, the scuffed black table-top, the tear in the vinyl seat covering. Neil reached forward to pick up his half-pint. He took a small sip. He was relaxed and leisurely, while my hands shook as I fumbled in my bag, which suddenly seemed to contain many more things than it had previously.

'Ooh, that's nice. Really cold,' he said.

My fingers found the edge of the envelope. Had I sealed it properly? I wondered. Would the cash fall out as I handed it to him, flutter around us and fall to the floor?

Neil took the envelope, folded it and slipped it into his back pocket.

'Nice doing business with you,' he said. 'Send my love to Dad.' He left, strolling out of the pub, giving the barman a small salute. 'Bye, mate.'

'Bye, Neil.'

I waited for him to leave.

I forced myself to remain sitting there, light a cigarette, take a sip of Neil's lager. It was not cold. He had lied.

I folded the newspaper in half and gripped it under my arm.

I smiled at the barman as I left, walking slowly. I did not run across the road. I waited for a gap in the traffic, proud of my sanguine self-control.

The red car clattered and rattled as we drove back to Cambridge on the motorway. I unfolded the newspaper, opened it. Between pages nine and ten there was a jiffy bag, already used. I opened it and looked inside, saw the plain white wraps of cocaine.

The red car clattered and rattled as though it might break apart.

It was only at this moment that I realized I had a choice, and my choices were what made me the person that I was, the person that I might become, that the wrong choices had consequences, and that life didn't just happen to you, you happened to it.

'Slow down,' I said.

But the music was too loud, so Dan didn't hear.

'Slow down!' I shouted, turning down the volume.

'What?'

'We have over three hundred pounds' worth of cocaine in the car with us. We don't want to get pulled over. Your dad's a fucking barrister.'

And we were both quiet as the flat East Anglian countryside sailed by.

29

2016, London

We are in our local branch of Sainsbury's, in the baking aisle.

'Can we have this?' says Minna, shoving two tubes of silver balls and some multi-coloured sprinkles in my face.

'And this?' says Hebe, finding the edible glitter spray.

'And this?' says Minna with a handful of packets of chocolate buttons.

'You can have whatever you want,' I say.

We are buying supplies to make a cake. The best cake ever.

The girls continue to fill the shopping basket with sugary treats, eyeing me with suspicion and wonder. Has she gone mad, is she going to change her mind, can this be real?

'Right, we've got everything we can here, let's go to the sweets,' I say.

Hebe and Minna run all the way to the sweet aisle. They grab packets of Smarties, mini marshmallows, sugar strings, jelly beans.

'Can we eat them now, can we eat them now?' shouts Minna.

'No, this is all for the special cake. When we've made

it, then you can eat the jelly beans. Then you can eat so many sweets you'll probably explode.'

Minna looks as though she is going to explode right here in front of me, in the middle of the supermarket.

I never could escape. When Dad moved out of home and went to live in Putney, finally giving me the space to start becoming my own person, I couldn't really keep away. I would visit him on Friday nights after I'd finished my homework. There would be a party, Julia and her friends, the young girls who lived with him (there were always a couple, making their beds on the floor out of sofa cushions), wine and cocaine. I went to Rome seeking order, an ancient civilization famous for its straight roads and laws, but Dad followed me there too. At Cambridge I tried to be prim, but found I had nothing to say to the gentle girls at the chocolate fondue evenings, gravitating instead to the naughty girls, the feisty ones, the messy ones; and I couldn't help but say, 'I know someone who can sort you out,' when they mentioned wanting to buy drugs (although I only actually bought drugs for other people the once. And, unlike my father, did not make a profit).

I thought I had finally found a refuge in my home, my family, my husband – a man so different to my father – my ordered life; but then the past came and bashed me on the head, dragging me back by my ankles.

I never could escape. I have to stop trying. Instead I have to integrate my past into my present in a way that will not destroy it.

I have told the world about my sister, but I still have not spoken to my children about her.

Candy needs to be part of our family. But how can I talk to my children about a nine-year-old girl who died in the night? I don't want my girls to think of Candy and feel afraid, I want them to think of a little girl who liked dancing and swimming, who painted colourful pictures, who loved pink clothes and sweets, a little girl who was full of life.

'I am going to tell you about my little sister,' I say when we get home from Sainsbury's. 'She was called Candy. She was four years younger than me, and when she was nine she caught a virus and she died. The virus is very rare, so you don't need to worry about it.'

They watch me as I speak. They look solemn.

'More than anything else Candy loved sweets and she loved things that were pink. She had a big pink coat that she loved so much she wore it all the time, even when it was sunny. Tomorrow is her birthday and the cake we are going to make is for her.'

'How many candles will it have?' asks Minna.

'I don't think we need to worry about candles. There won't be enough room for them anyway. There will be too many sweets.'

The next day I make the cake, two chocolate sponges stuck together with chocolate icing. I make triple the amount of pink frosting recommended and slather this over the cake with a red plastic spatula as my girls watch, gripping the edge of the table. Then they get to work, sprinkling, attaching, spraying, lacing the cake with what seems like all the sweets in the world. The icing sags and is soon completely overwhelmed by this multicoloured medley of sugary insanity. It is the maddest, most over-the-top cake ever seen. I invite my mother over and she pops one of her diabetes tablets in preparation. I cut thick slices, the icing oozing, Smarties and jelly beans tumbling, and we eat, finishing the slices, feeling sick and high afterwards.

We decide to make the cake every year.

'I think that is a really good idea,' says Hebe.

A few months later I go to Minna's parents' evening. I sit on a small plastic chair intended for a six-year-old and Minna's teacher shows me a piece of work she has done. It is a drawing of Candy and a description of her, written phonetically, the little girl who loved sweets and who died, my mummy's sister.

I try not to cry as I look at what Minna has made. It is not that I am sad. The tears are because I am happy. I have created a memory of Candy for my children. Sweet and pink and a bit bonkers.

30

2005, London

I could never believe my father would die. He was a bull of a man, built for endurance, a happy god with a big belly and a wolf smile, gulping wine as though it was water, sucking so hard on his cigarette that he made the filter soggy, snorting two lines of cocaine just to hoover his flat on a Saturday morning.

Once he was very proud of himself because a doctor had examined him and told him that all the cocaine had cleared his lungs of tar, that the amphetamines had made his heart strong. Dad was so pleased with the awe this young doctor felt for his miraculous sixty-year-old body. The best bit was when the doctor said that the only other case he had ever seen like it was Keith Richards. 'Me and Keith, it's just me and Keith! Two old rockers,' Dad said. It was as if the drugs, the alcohol, the smoking, had made him healthier. Which sounds impossible, but if you'd met him you'd have believed it.

My mother would sometimes say, 'It is going to be so hard on you when he goes,' and I would say, 'Yeah,' without commitment or concern. Her heavy words were light to me because she didn't understand what I understood.

That it was never going to happen. She didn't know what I knew.

I am not sure whether this myth of immortality was his or mine. Either way, I took it more seriously than he did. For him everything was a joke. Even death.

Dad hadn't even told me about his latest visit to the hospital. The first I knew was when he phoned me at work on a Thursday afternoon. We were due to have dinner that night at Pucci's, a pizza restaurant on the King's Road where we always went because we'd known the owners for years and because Dad liked going back to the same places, again and again, the same way he liked watching the same films and telling the same stories, again and again.

'All right, my darling, it's your old dad,' he said, sounding as if he was lazing on a sun lounger somewhere exotic, even though it was late November and already dark outside, black branches thrashing in the wind.

'Hi,' I said. 'Seven thirty, right? Bella is coming too.' I was being short with him, but I had a lot to do and this conversation was superfluous. All the arrangements had been made. I would relax when I saw him, when the wine was in front of me. I was looking forward to it.

'Great. Oh yeah, you've got a minute, right, because I've just been to the hospital. That new one, Royal Brompton, it's like a hotel in there. Anyway, it was just meant to be a check-up. Scans and stuff. But the guy said that I have an, an anurarism.' He paused; then he said it more carefully, as though he was reading from a prompt, 'An aortic aneurism. I think it's quite serious!'

I already had the phone lodged between my ear and my shoulder, hunched to keep it secure while I typed the words into my computer, the sounds of the newsroom fading, so the only thing I could hear was my father breathing, the laboured rasping amplified and made more dangerous by the hollow plastic handset, the coiled wire, the distance between us, all the way to a satellite floating beyond the earth's atmosphere and back.

I read quickly. A dilation of the aorta which could result in sudden rupture and massive internal bleeding.

'Fucking hell, Dad, this is serious. What did the doctor say, what are they going to do, where are you now, are you at the hospital?'

'No, mate, they sent me away. With my aneurism!' He laughed, and then coughed. He was trying to make it sound fun, as though he had a new pet, 'my aneurism!', but I could tell by the thin pull in his voice that he was scared. I heard him light a cigarette, the sudden intake of breath, the slow outward whoosh. I had read enough in those few seconds to know that smoking was one of the things that could cause a rupture: smoking, drinking, unhealthy living. A massive rupture that would cause instant death.

'Fucking hell, Dad,' I said again.

The sub-editor who had been standing by my desk, unnoticed, placed two proofs on my keyboard.

'I've really got to go. I'll see you later,' I said.

'OK, love you!'

'Yeah.'

I felt too scared to talk, fizzy and numb at the same

time. I put down the phone. I could still feel the pressure of the handset against my ear. It must have left a red mark because I had been pushing it against my head so hard.

I looked at the proofs of the magazine, pretended to read, my eyes sliding across the letters without registering anything. I ticked my initials and handed the pages to the editor sitting next to me.

I spent the next two hours researching aortic aneurisms, approaching it professionally, as if this was an act of work rather than heartache, delving deeper, taking notes, discounting websites that looked too home-spun. I left the office with my eyes gristly from staring at my computer. I had not learnt much more than I had in those first few seconds.

My father's aortic artery had ballooned in one fatal spot. The walls of this part of the vessel grew thinner with every heartbeat; the faster and more intense the heartbeat, the thicker and more syrupy the blood, the more likely the balloon would burst. There would be no advance warning of this calamitous internal explosion. It could just happen. Any time. Or not. There was no way of knowing. All I knew was that he would have to change the way he'd always lived, the lying on the sofa drinking half a bottle of vodka while he watched films, the eating of all four crème caramels in a pack in one sitting, the duty-free multi-packs of Silk Cut that would be finished in a week ('Here, have a pack,' Dad would say to friends), the beer before lunch and the Baileys before bed. Otherwise my father, my happy immortal, would die. And that was unthinkable, impossible.

The thing I realized, as I walked from High Street Kensington to the King's Road, my hair whipping in the wind, was that I had to take charge. That was what Dad wanted. That was why he had called. He lived alone now, in an ex-council flat in Battersea – he and Julia had separated not long after I left university – and he knew this task was beyond him. He also knew that I was rigorous enough, bossy enough, and that I loved him enough, to take on the job of saving his life.

I called Bella on the way to explain. 'It might be a bit weird. You don't have to come if you don't want to.'

'Don't be silly. Of course I'm coming. I'm nearly there. Poor you. Your poor dad. This is shit. We'll make it fun for him.'

They were both already there when I reached the restaurant: Bella's hair swept behind her shoulders, a floaty white thrift-shop top, unseasonal tan; Dad looking smart in an ironed shirt, with a glass of red wine filled to the brim and a cigarette in his hand.

I kissed them both and sat down. They looked so relaxed, as though nothing had changed, nothing was scary, their faces warm in the candlelight. I felt I was in a different film, anxious and absorbed, not wanting to take my coat off, gripping my bag on my lap.

Our friend who owned the restaurant was not working that night, and the place wasn't busy. A waiter put a plate of pizzette on the table for us, mini pizzas with tomato sauce and olives. I let my hands unclasp, put my bag on the floor, drank some wine.

'Busy day?' said Dad.

'Sort of,' I replied. I couldn't work out why I felt angry with him, so I ate one of the little pizzas, and then another, and one more.

'Crazy news!' he said, waving his fag in the air as though he was conjuring some sort of magic.

Bella laughed. 'Oh, Gav,' she said and put her hand on his forearm.

'I suppose,' I said.

I took off my coat, let it slump on the back of the chair, stiffened my spine for the speech I was about to deliver.

'So, Dad, I did a lot of research today, and—'

'See, I told you,' he said to Bella.

I tried to breathe. He'd always found my studiousness inexplicable, always thought it was funny, how a man like him could create a child like me.

'This is not a joke,' I said.

He stopped laughing and looked at me, the pouches of skin under his eyes grey and saggy. He had just shaved and his face looked bloated without his stubble. He held his mouth tightly pursed, merriment contained just for the moment. This was his 'I'm concentrating' face.

'Dad. This thing, the thing in you, it could kill you at any moment. You have to be really careful from now on. Basically, you have a choice: grandchildren or cocaine. Because if you keep taking coke, you are not going to live long enough to meet your grandchildren.'

'Are you pregnant?' he said, mischief making his mouth quiver even as he tried to maintain a serious expression.

'For fuck's sake,' I said, looking away, making my eyes wide to keep them dry. I reached for his cigarettes. As I brought a fag to my mouth Dad swiped the Zippo from the table and offered me a light.

'I am not pregnant,' I said, inhaling nicotine calm. 'I am just saying that maybe in the next few years I might be having kids. I would really like for you to be around for that. And if you keep on the way you have been, you probably won't be.'

'I know, I'm sorry. Come on, G, give me a hug,' he said. He shifted his chair around to face me and pulled me to him. It was awkward, I had to hold my hand with the cigarette out to one side, and my glasses were dislodged, pressing against my face painfully as he hugged harder, the feel of his jumper soft against my cheek.

'Always get cashmere, so when someone touches your arm or your back, they'll just assume you're rich,' he once told me.

I loved his hugs really. They are the thing I remember about him most.

I pulled free and the young Italian waiter approached. Dad fancied spaghetti carbonara, but I said no, he should have the chicken breast with vegetables, which was healthier, better for his heart.

'We might as well start tonight,' I said.

'That's right, darling, this is what I need,' he said. He was chuckling with his shoulders and belly. The strange thing was that he seemed more delighted than scared. I think he was so happy that I was willing to take on this role, policing his habits, an active and demanding demonstration of my devotion, that it counterbalanced his fear, or whatever it was that he felt when he considered his own death. I began to relax. If he would listen to me, if he would let me take control of this, then we might have a chance.

'I am going to call every day,' I said. 'And I want to come with you to the next doctor's appointment. I have lots of questions.'

He looked at me with shining, proud eyes. Here I was, his serious daughter. Hermione, he used to call me, and Saffy before that. If anyone could sort him out, I was the one.

'They're not going to know what's hit 'em!'

I had to go to the loo and when I came back the conversation had moved on. Bella was talking about an ex-boyfriend who had moved to Ibiza and was Kate Moss's driver. Dad was expressing his admiration for Moss's party stamina, although, he said, she was too skinny for him. 'I like a handful, if you know what I mean.' But it was fine, I had said what I needed to say, made my point, really made it stick with the grandchildren thing. Dad loved children. He would definitely want to be a part of his grandchildren's life, if only to be a bad influence, feed them too many sweets and let them watch too much telly, try to make them love him more than they loved my mother. He wouldn't want to miss out on that game. I knew I was using low tactics, but the severity of the situation demanded them.

Our food came and Dad stole a slice of my American Hot pizza, but he didn't eat much of his chicken, which he said was too dry. We had finished the first bottle of wine quickly and were now nearly at the end of the second. I was drunk, my anxiety dulled by wine and cig-arettes, by music and gossip. It was going to be OK; he would listen to me. I would talk to the doctor, find out about the possibilities, operations that could be per-formed, regimes that needed to be adhered to. Now I knew what needed to be done, now I had formulated a plan, I felt less scared. So it seemed fine, suddenly, for Dad to order three flaming sambucas and a plate of quivering tiramisu. This was his final night of fun – he couldn't die in front of my eyes. I knew that couldn't happen to me a second time.

Could it?

No. While I was here watching, my father would not die. So he stuck his teaspoon into the dessert and his eyes clouded with pleasure as he ate the creamy pudding and drank the sticky-sweet, still-warm liquor. This was the life.

Dad gave me the cash for a cab home, pulling two twenty-pound notes out of his wallet, even though he wasn't rich any more. But he liked the gesture, pretend-ing to be wealthy made him believe that he was.

In the cab back home to Brixton, where I was now liv-ing in an ex-council flat with Mike, I got a call from Bella.

'That was nice,' I said, feeling just drunk enough and enjoying the view out of the cab window, the shimmer-ing shop fronts, the pre-Christmas glitter that made even South London showy.

'I have to tell you something,' she said.

'What?'

'When you were in the loo your dad asked me if I

wanted a line of coke. That's what he was doing all those times he went to the loo. He said, "Don't tell her, whatever you do, don't get me into trouble."'

Oh, I could imagine it. He would lean forward, press his forefinger to his nose, wink. He loved a secret, loved a tiny betrayal. *Do you want a line?*

I sat back in the seat. He would never change. At least I could trust him on that.

We went to the hospital together a month later. I made sure that we got there early. I knew that this just meant that we would have to spend longer in the waiting room, with its plastic moulded chairs and strip lighting, sick people slumped all around, breathing out germs and decay. But I didn't want to be flustered. I had to be calm, so I could ask all the questions on my list in a measured, unhurried fashion.

'Slow down for your old man,' said Dad as we walked the short distance from the bus stop to the hospital. He was using a walking stick, a slender and pliant dark wood cane, the bone handle attached with a strip of leather and carved with a delicate pomegranate. This was the first time I'd seen him use a stick. He said it was the old injury. The metal pins he'd had put in his leg after he got run over in Marbella now ached constantly, rather than just before it was about to rain.

I didn't know where he'd got the walking stick. It looked fancy. I assumed he'd nicked it from one of his rich friends.

I slowed down.

'You're always in such a hurry. It'll still be there, you know, if we get there five minutes later.'

'I know. Sorry, Dad.'

'Look around a bit more, enjoy life.'

I checked us in at reception and we found some seats near a television screen. There was no sound, but Dad still wanted to be able to watch it. He stretched his legs out in front of him and sighed.

'I hate hospitals. You know that, don't you, G? Just put a cushion over my face before it comes to this, promise me.'

I looked at him. His skin was damp and grey, there were liver spots on his hands and his teeth were stained brown at the gums. His eyelashes were short and his eyebrows were sparse. I finally understood that it was unlikely to come to this.

At night, by candlelight, his face came alive.

He hadn't done anything I'd asked him to do. He hadn't stopped drinking or smoking; he hadn't stopped eating ice-cream from the tub or snorting cocaine. In fact, he was behaving worse than ever. At dinner he would choose the fattiest, most calorific dishes, licking grease off his fingers like a later Roman emperor, gargling expensive red wine, using a dessertspoon to eat a whole chocolate mousse in three mouthfuls. He had taken to adding whisky to his coffee and smoking cigars after dinner, reclining in decadent splendour, holding his belly as it split his denim shirt.

He found the knowledge that he could die at any moment a fantastic liberation. Could it be this slick of foie gras, this cigarette, this gulp of brandy Alexander, this huge line of very pure, perfectly white cocaine? And how much more delicious all these deadly indulgences were with the knowledge that this might be the last toot, the last sip, the last taste. He wasn't scared. In fact, I had never seen him happier. He relished the delicious wickedness of his new roulette game. And I gave up trying to stop him killing himself. I joined in. I didn't want to regret not having fun with him until the very end. We'd planned to go to a new bar in Battersea Square for strawberry daiquiris after his hospital appointment. Neil was going to meet us.

'Mr Hodge,' called a man who looked about the same age as me. Dark hair, white coat, fairly handsome.

We followed him into a small office. There were clear plastic trays on the shelves and a big, old-fashioned computer on the desk. The consultant pressed a key on his keyboard and the thing whirred into life. He read what was on the screen.

'So, Mr Hodge, you came in for some tests a few weeks ago?'

I hated the way they were never prepared. The doctor hadn't even read Dad's history before we'd come in.

'Yes, that's right, and my father was diagnosed with an aortic aneurism. What we really want to talk about is next steps. I have been researching stents and although this is serious surgery I think it would be the best option, considering the severity of my father's condition. I have to say I am a little surprised that we've had to wait so long for this follow-up appointment, under the circumstances.'

I stopped talking and took a cool and imperious breath. I could feel the pleasure glowing from my father.

I didn't even have to look at him to know how much he had enjoyed my speech.

The consultant looked a little flustered, as well he might. He stared again at his computer and did something with his mouse, scrolling up and down.

'Um . . .' he said.

'What we would both really like is a time-frame,' I said, interrupting his hesitation. 'I am sure you can understand that this has all been very upsetting.' I took my notepad from my bag and put it on the desk, flipped it open and held my biro poised in a way that I hoped would be really quite intimidating.

'Come on, darling, give the doc a break, they're really busy here,' said Dad. He winked at the consultant, as if to say: Women! Unbelievable!

It annoyed me that he always had to be the fun guy.

'Well, yes, but . . .' The consultant was still looking at his screen as he spoke. 'I really can't find any reference here to an aneurism. What the notes are suggesting is that there was an anomaly with the test results. So what we actually need to do is to find a time for Mr Hodge to do some more tests. I'm really sorry about that; I realize it is an inconvenience. But there really is nothing here to cause concern. Everything else seems very straightforward, as far as I can see.'

The consultant looked up at me and smiled in a way that I imagine he thought was charming.

I looked down at my notes and set my mouth in a hard, straight line.

An anomaly.

I knew my father was dyslexic, but this really was taking the piss.

An anomaly.

Dad laughed. 'You're kidding! That's brilliant. Isn't that brilliant, G?'

'Yes,' I said.

My father seemed tired when we left the hospital. He said he didn't fancy strawberry daiquiris after all. He said he just wanted to go home. So we went back and lay on his sofas and watched television in companionable silence. Him on his sofa, me on mine.

31

2016, London

'But you remember the time we took Candida and two of her friends to the Windmill Theatre for her birthday? You were so brilliant in the car, you entertained them the whole way there, telling them stories.'

My mother repeats this anecdote every time we see each other. She is trying to help, I know that, trying to trigger my memories of Candy. But more than anything she is worrying me: the diabetes seems to be clouding her mind. Sometimes she is just as sharp as ever, but more often than not she repeats herself, gets confused, mixes things up.

'No, I don't remember that, I'm sorry, Mum,' I say.

I don't say what I am thinking, which is: 'You told me that last week, and the week before, and the week before that.' I don't say, 'Is that the only memory of Candy you have left?'

I don't say this because I hate to see my mother upset. I hate to see anyone upset, but particularly my mother, not just because she is my mother, but because it reminds me too much of the time after Candy died and because she hurts so easily.

When I told Mum that I was starting to see a therapist, she cried.

'I am worried that you will talk about me and what it was like after Candy. I know I pulled away from you, but you have to understand, it hurt so much, and I couldn't bear to hurt like that again. It was all I could do.'

Mum stopped drinking when Dad went into rehab in 1984. She joined Alcoholics Anonymous and completed the twelve-step programme, learning the serenity prayer by heart and making me learn it too. She was very active in AA (before and) after Candy died. She became a sponsor, looking after young women in the early days of sobriety. They would call at all hours of the day and night. I would hear Mum murmuring softly to them, comforting them, guiding them. It made me furious. I hated their weakness. I wanted to pick up the phone and shout, 'Have a fucking drink if you want one that badly.'

Maybe I was so angry because it felt as if all her care was being given to them, not me. My mother's fear of the darkness in our home, the drugs in the sitting room when I was a little girl and again when I was a teenager, the chaos, the wrongness of everything, made her unable to see what was happening.

But when she did finally see, when she held the evidence in her hands, she threw Dad out without hesitation. If Mum had not done that, nothing would have changed. She was the one who spoke to my headmistress about why I had done badly in my GCSEs and why we needed help financially (Dad had declared himself bankrupt and was unable to pay his half of my school fees). She was the one who persuaded the school to let me take the

A-levels I wanted and to give me a bursary. She was the one who made our home a safe, clean place while I studied for my A-levels, knocking on the door every morning with a cup of tea to wake me up in time to get ready for school, for my exams, for my Saturday job.

She had been the one who pushed for me to go to a 'good' secondary school in the first place, taking me to the open days, arranging a tutor. She had been a bright little girl, just like me, passing her eleven-plus and going to grammar school, but her father hadn't encouraged her. He refused to help her with maths, even though he was an accountant and helped her elder brother. My mother always felt unloved (she was an unwanted third child, an unsuccessful abortion). She would hide in a cupboard when it was time to go to school, but only because she wanted to be found. Her parents never looked for her, never even noticed she was missing, and when she was fourteen she was asked to leave school because of non-attendance. She became a model and always got the bridal slot at the end of the fashion show because she looked so pure, white-blonde hair and violet eyes. She hated being looked at and drank too much, the wine softening her painful edges.

She was there on the morning when the letter came offering me a place at Cambridge.

For many years I was prickly with Mum. I found her inside-out grief hard to witness and her religious zeal hard to understand. It was easier with Dad. He never required me to be honest, only complicit, which is much more fun, and fun is what you think you need when the world is falling down around you. Not brokenness and introversion. I realize now that what my mother was trying to do was to deal with her grief, to engage with it and accept it, rather than bury it or ignore it or drown it in wine. She wanted to talk about how she felt; we preferred to drink and take drugs so we didn't feel at all. It is only as I have got older that I have realized her path was the healthier one.

My relationship with my mother has become much easier since the birth of my children. Mum helped look after both my girls when they were small, enabling me to go back to work. Once she recklessly freewheeled down our steep road after a night of snow so that Mike and I would not miss a day in the office. She loved looking after babies once more – a second chance. She liked to take them to Costa Coffee on the high street for babyccinos, and would spend hours playing cuddly toy catch with Hebe. No one was more moved than her at how like Candy Minna looked.

But I still find my mother's vulnerability hard to witness.

'Shall I come and see you for lunch next week?' I say. 'Just the two of us?'

We are rarely alone together.

'That would be lovely,' Mum says.

So much has been unsaid between us for so long it feels like the scary, challenging parts of our history have become ossified, hardened, that they will need to be chipped away at to be released, a hard and painful process requiring sharp tools and the possibility of injury. How can I ask the questions that have been lodged in me for so long that they are a part of me, how can I find a way for Mum to hear the questions without feeling as though I am judging her, or answer them without dissolving into sadness?

But it is my job to ask difficult questions. I do this all the time, interviewing celebrities about their complicated childhoods and professional struggles. I don't swerve probing questions when there is a Dictaphone on the table. So maybe this is the answer. If I frame my conversation with my mother as an interview it will be easier for both of us; the act of recording will give us the distance from the past we need to return to it and the Dictaphone will be a non-judgemental third party. I will be the interviewer and my mother will be the subject.

An interview with Jan Hodge, conducted at Yeha restaurant in Norwood Junction

Do you remember when you first met Dad? You were standing on the Embankment, weren't you, after a party, and Dad picked you up in his Campervan?

That's right. There were eight of us models standing in full evening dress trying to hitch a lift and he was the only man with enough balls to stop. He took us to the Roebuck pub on the King's Road and all his friends gravitated towards us. I didn't speak to anyone; I just stood there and laughed. Then he took me to Tramp [the nightclub in Mayfair], and I was wearing a very low-cut frock, and you know when you go down the stairs at Tramp there's an area where people sit and he placed me there because there was a light that shone directly on to me. He placed me there to show off my breasts to everybody.

Did you think he was funny?
Yes, I thought he was funny and I liked him, so much so that I slept downstairs on the floor at home in Woodford Green in case he rang after that first date.

Was he the first person you fell in love with?
I definitely had strong feelings for him from the beginning.

The thing that I have always thought was that you were such an introvert and he was such an extrovert, that you felt shy, whereas Dad could do all the talking, and that was part of the attraction.
Yes, that's right.

And you shared a sense of humour.
We did.

And you were both from the suburbs and inhabiting this glamorous Chelsea world but not quite part of it, only allowed to be part of it because of your beauty and talent.
We were both very good at what we did. And yes, that sort of sums us up. We really were in love. Your dad was fairly brassic when I met him, but he always took me to nice places.

He always believed in the show, didn't he?

Yes, it was always about the show. He used to take me to lovely restaurants on the King's Road when we first met.

And were you trying to get pregnant?

No, but I think your dad was trying. He wasn't at all sad when I told him I was pregnant. There was never any question of him trying to back away or back out of it. He asked me to go and live with him pretty quickly after I told him. And I did.

And did you know that he was using drugs at the time?

I didn't know anything about drugs when I met your father. I'd never had a drug. I'd never indulged in such things. Never had the urge. I think I'd taken one drag of a reefer once. I didn't like it. He actually asked me to take drugs with him the day after we got married. You'd gone down to my sister.

So he waited until you were married before he revealed that part of himself?

Yes, he saved that until after we got married.

And what was the drug that he wanted to take with you?

Cocaine.

And what did you say?

I did it.

And were you on your honeymoon?

No, we were just in Chelsea in the flat for a few days and your father went demented. He had a really good time. He thought it was great.

I think the other thing that Dad did was that he compartmentalized things. So to him his lies weren't lies, they were just compartments.

That's right. It was interesting because we did discuss what was important to us, where marriage was concerned, before we got married. And it was fidelity. I was faithful right the way through the marriage, and he was until Twinkle [my mother's name for Julia]. And there were such extenuating circumstances. Any man who had given his daughter the kiss of life and had water and blood come back into his mouth and then she died was not going to be normal, were they? And I've always given that leeway for his behaviour, but I just couldn't live with it, and you didn't want to.

It's really hard, isn't it, trying to forgive someone for doing something unforgivable and knowing the context for those actions, and also still loving them at the same time.

I never stopped loving your father, and he did love me. But he was an addict and that was all there was to it. The best years of our marriage were when he got clean and I got sober. We had great times.

And it is such a tragedy that Candy died, for so many reasons, but one reason was that when she died that ended the family.

That's right. I can understand that he never got over it, what happened that night.

So, let's go back again. You got pregnant, got married, had me.
And we were both very happy; we both exchanged the same sentiment to each other: thank you, for you.

And you were living in Elm Park Mansions, and you were working as a model, and Dad had his hairdressing salon in the King's Road, Gotama, which he opened after he came back from Marbella.
Yes, and everything was all right, but it wasn't all right for very long, because he soon had money problems because he was just not a good businessman. Gotama went down quite quickly because your father had started using [taking heroin] quite heftily.

When did you become aware that his using was causing problems?
When he went to bed and stayed there for three days. You were still about two. That was when he came to understand that Gotama was going to go under. He was depressed. It was a loss.

It was how he responded to loss and pain, wasn't it, seeking oblivion?
Yes. But he rallied from that and started to do freelance hairdressing and he was doing well. We sold Elm Park Mansions and moved over the river.

When do you think he started dealing drugs?
After Candy was born.

Oh, really, not before?

He could have done it on the side without me knowing. But it was when Candy was four and you were eight that the police came.

And that was the first time you were really aware of what was going on?

No, I knew before, but I used to get drunk and go to bed.

Because you didn't want to think about what was going on in the sitting room?

That's right, and you used to go out and clean up after them.

And did you know that I was doing that?

I did. And it used to really worry me. These days you and Candida would have been taken from us. You should have been then, to be honest. Although I am really glad you weren't.

Me too. It's a strange thing, because you think: Where were social services? But actually I am glad that social services didn't intervene.

We could both still put a show on and behave like normal people.

I had clothes, I had food, I went to school.

You had toys, you were clean, all of those things. And the same with Candy.

Part of what I've been trying to do is unravel everything and put it in order in my own head, because it is so complex and complicated. I have been thinking about you and Dad and the things that brought you together and the things that pulled you apart, and the differences in your responses to things, and one of the things that I have found hard to understand was how these things were allowed to continue [I am referring here to when I was sitting up with my father and the junkies] but I suppose you were thinking: We are just about getting by, we are just about holding on, and I am scared of the things that are going on in the living room, but I can't stop him doing them.

That's right. I was a functioning alcoholic. And it was quite a terrifying thing because I knew that when people are dealing, other people will come and beat up the whole family, you know. There were things like that I was really terrified of.

I do remember one time someone coming and banging on the door and trying to break in and Dad holding the door shut and shouting fuck off.

Oh, I didn't know that. I don't remember that. But I suppose it would have been someone wanting money or drugs or something. I mean, your father's heart was good.

And what was it like when Candy was born? What was home like?

Well, as I have said to you, because she was the first child of his who was actually born in wedlock, your father was besotted with her. He was weirdly old-fashioned. When we found out about Twinkle, he said to me: Candy would have understood. It's the first thing he said. And I said, Don't be so bloody stupid; she would have kicked you in the balls. I think he thought Candy was his soul mate, and I think that is why he couldn't recover at all. Not to say that he didn't love you, because he most certainly did, he adored you, but there was this special thing, because he was so stupidly old-fashioned. It never made a blind bit of difference to me. I rarely remembered that was even the case, and anyway you had your father on your birth certificate and everything.

And what was I like as a child?

You were quite independent, but you just enjoyed normal things, you enjoyed being read to. I always took you off to mother-and-baby club and you always enjoyed that. You always had little friends. I always thought after Candida died that you were sort of God's gift because any other child would have made life even harder.

This conversation is a revelation. It changes the way I think about both of my parents, how ill suited they were, and yet how suited, the similarities of their backgrounds, of their outlooks, their childish sense of humour, the balance of his extroversion with her shyness, his deceit with her honesty. They were beautiful and young and in love and because they were in love they made a family. Their meeting might have been a matter of chance, but having a child, that was choice.

I always felt loved. I went to friends' homes where there was so much material wealth, so much security, so much normality, so much of what I desired, and yet often not enough love. Perhaps that was why I always wanted to come home. Our scrappy, mad, chaotic family was filled with love and fun and when it was good there was nowhere else I wanted to be.

32

2009, London

It was strange to be in the flat without him.

I sat on the sofa, his sofa, the one with the best view of the television. I brought my feet up, leant my back against the armrest, sitting in the place he always sat, settling in the space made by his body.

It was morning. I was here by myself. I didn't want anyone else with me. They kept calling. I looked at their names but I didn't answer.

The flat still smelt of the food Mike had ordered the night before, the silver foil dishes lined up on the coffee table between us, the meat curries cooling and congealing. Someone broke off an edge of poppadom and chewed it. There is an instinct to feed the newly bereaved. I still had the KitKat that a friend had bought me after I got the call.

Maybe I would lose weight.

'You should see him,' said Sarah, still his best friend after all these years, although he'd stopped calling her Lady Sarah. 'He's in the bathroom.'

I didn't want to.

She held my arm, trying to pull me up the stairs. 'You should see him.'

'I don't want to. I can't. Maybe in a bit.'

'He was on the loo,' she said, her voice raspy. 'The door was locked. I bashed and bashed at it with that fucking bronze elephant of his. He was meant to be meeting us for dinner, for Chrissy's birthday. He was meant to be collecting the birthday cake. He didn't answer my calls all day. So I came round.'

I wailed like an animal when I got the call from Sarah. The whole office turned to see what was making the terrible sound.

They led me outside, holding me by the elbows. They'd called Mike, who was working in the same building. The KitKat was in the pocket of my velvet coat. Mike hailed a black cab for us.

'I am disintegrating,' I said to him.

I understood what it meant then: falling to pieces. That is how it feels. We are so fragile, we humans, our cells bound together by subtle energies. We come apart easily.

It was Friday. I sat in his spot, on his sofa, my legs up in front of me, the television on, daytime television, *Cash in the Attic*, something mindless; he loved that sort of thing. I didn't know where to start. His body was at Chelsea and Westminster Hospital. The paramedics had arrived while we sat there with the curries.

'You should look at him, this is your last chance,' Sarah had said.

'I don't want to.'

We sat in silence as the paramedics banged and bashed around, getting his body out of the loo and on to the stretcher on the small landing in front of the bathroom. They carried him downstairs. I stared at the curries, brown and lumpen. They carried him out of the flat, taking him down in the lift to the waiting ambulance. There was no urgency.

Now I sat in his spot. On the table was a bronze tray arranged with his knick-knacks, ammonites and shells, fake jade, strange ephemera. There was a ring; it was soft gold set with a large lapis lazuli, the blue flecked with tiny particles of gold. I had admired it before.

'It's really old, that,' Dad had said. He didn't tell me where he had got it from; he'd probably stolen it from one of his rich friends. Seen it, desired it, taken it, reasoning that they had so much they wouldn't even notice it was gone.

I slid the ring on to the third finger of my right hand.

What would I do with all his stuff? Where should I begin?

His body. They had taken his body to the hospital mortuary. He hated hospitals; he never wanted to end up in one. I could sense his impatience to leave that cold place where no one looked their best, where no one could even pretend that life was grand.

Put a cushion over my face before it comes to this.

I found a funeral directors on the internet. I called them and began to make the arrangements. Set the wheels in motion.

It was as complicated as organizing a wedding, but you only have two weeks to do everything and you are ruined with heartbreak.

I took my favourite paintings off his living-room walls, called a cab and took them home with me. That night I smelt of dust and despair when I sang baby Hebe to sleep.

He'd come to the hospital to see her when she was just born; he turned up stinking of fags, eating a sandwich, spitting it all over me, my sheets, my new baby.

'Do you know what, it's as bad as being black, being left-handed,' he said.

'For fuck's sake, Dad, that is such a stupid thing to say,' I whispered.

I was in a shared ward in King's College Hospital. Every other woman in that ward was either African or British Caribbean, as were so many of the brilliant and kind nurses who looked after me.

'But it's true!'

'Just shut up!'

He sat on the end of my bed and cradled Hebe. 'Aren't you lovely?' he said.

The last time I saw him he came to Crystal Palace to have lunch with the two of us. We went to the cheap Italian place. He had finally accepted that he wasn't rich.

'I wish I was a swallow,' he said. 'I hate the winter. I wish I could fly away and spend it somewhere hot, and then I could come back here in the summer. Or maybe I could be a hedgehog, then I could hibernate it all away.'

I hadn't realized that he was in pain, that he felt ill, that he was feeling his mortality. As he walked away from us towards the train station, Hebe, who was attached to my front in a baby-carrier, kept straining round my shoulder to look at him.

'What are you looking at, you funny little thing?'

I turned and I watched Dad walk away, whistling.

He died two days later of pulmonary complications.

I called a cab and took the paintings back to his flat. I realized that I wanted to be able to sit in his home as it had been for as long as I could.

I spoke to the female priest at St Mary The Boltons, the church around the corner from my old primary school, the church where we had held the funeral service for my sister, twenty years earlier.

'Of course your father can have his funeral here,' she said. 'You are part of this community.'

I spotted a Post-It note attached to the notepad when I put down the phone. 'Thank you, Gav', it said. The note was written in pencil, in what looked like my father's handwriting.

Most likely it had been written by Dad's friend Tim, who had stayed over on the last night, sleeping in the spare room, leaving in the morning before Dad woke up and died.

Thank you, Gav, for letting me stay the night; thank you, Gav, for putting on a really fun party; thank you, Gav, for the drugs and the good times.

But it really looked like my father's handwriting.

Perhaps he had left the note for me. Perhaps he knew.

Thank you, Gav, for forgiving me for all the things I did.

I took the Post-It note and stuck it in my wallet.

Sarah came to the flat. We sat opposite each other on his sofas, the paintings rehung on the walls above us, the knick-knacks in the tray on the table between us. He was dead but his flat was unchanged. The only things that were different were that the lock on the bathroom door was broken and the ring I had taken was still on my finger.

Sarah was tall and too thin in jeans and white plimsolls. She scratched her arms compulsively and talked about the parasites that lived under her skin. She was Dad's best friend and his best customer. He still did her hair and still sold her drugs, grinding Pro Plus tablets into the cocaine he sold her and charged her too much for. He told me this was because he cared about her and the adulterated cocaine was better for her health.

'He wanted to be buried with Candy's ashes, he told me that,' she said.

I'd never spoken to my father about his wishes.

If he was going to be buried, it would have to be in Brompton Cemetery, close to the King's Road.

'I'm a King's Road cowboy,' he used to say.

They only do burials once a week at Brompton. You have to pay upfront. There are fewer than a hundred plots left. Marchesa Casati and Bernard Levin are buried there, Polish fighter pilots and suffragettes. He'd fit right in.

The cemetery director was an Australian who only

had one arm, the loose end of his green linen shirt folded up neatly. He showed me the plot where I could bury my father. It was near to the pathway, so the joggers and the new mothers pushing their prams would be able to see him. A social spot, with Chelsea football ground just behind the wall. He'd be able to hear the crowds on match days.

I spoke to the man my father rented his flat from. He was called Anthony. 'There are ten days left on this month,' he said. 'Everything will have to be cleared out after that.'

Mike came to the flat with me the next day. He went into my father's bedroom and washed out the champagne bucket that was on the floor next to his bed. It was half filled with yellowish bile. Had my father vomited, got up, gone to the loo, died as he sat there? Had he felt ill, had he known he was dying?

Mike left me to get home to our baby.

I went to my dad's bedroom and I lay on his bed. His bedclothes smelt of stale sweat.

There was an old wooden dressing table with a grey marble top. The dressing table had lots of drawers into which he had stuffed photographs, letters, undeveloped rolls of film. In one drawer I found a cache of photographs of his ex-girlfriend, Julia. He had kept them all this time. Maybe he really had been in love with her, I thought as I sat on the floor and looked through them, unsticking them from each other, arranging them into neat piles. Maybe she had been the great love of his life. She'd certainly made him very happy. But after six years together she left him for a younger man. It broke Dad's heart. He listened to Bryan Adams '(Everything I Do) I Do It For You' on a loop that whole summer.

I wondered if I should try to contact her and tell her that he had died, invite her to the funeral. I had not always been kind to Julia, I knew that. I had blamed her more than him for what had happened, when really he was the one at fault. He was the adult, and she'd had a hard life too. But still, they had not been in touch for years and I decided I did not want to invite her.

Maranda flew in from Los Angeles, leaving her eighteen-month-old daughter, Biba. She'd been in London only a couple of weeks earlier for work. She was a successful hairdresser now, booked for luxury advertising campaigns and fashion magazines, travelling the world as part of the entourage for big Hollywood films. Maranda, Dad and I had met at Claridge's hotel, where she was staying. Dad was so proud of us, I was deputy editor of *ES Magazine*, Maranda had an expense account which meant she could pick up the drinks tab. Dad ordered champagne and gave her his gold chain, something she had always coveted.

'Here you are, my darling. But don't get too hung up on it. Don't worry if you lose it, it's only a necklace.'

Maranda could only stay for a couple of days; she had to go back to LA before the funeral because she had been booked for a commercial. We sat in his flat together, sisters who did not know each other, and I told her to take anything she wanted. She took a lot of Dad's hairdressing equipment, including the big bronze boot that he'd kept his hairbrushes in when he had the salon in Knightsbridge.

'I cleaned this so many fucking times, I have to have it.'

Chryssoulla came over. She had been with us on the holiday in Tunisia, the daughter of friends who had a jewellery shop on the same street as Dad's salon. She was Candy's age. She and Dad were great friends; he was like a second father to her – he had done her hair for her wedding. She lived in Athens now and it was pure chance that she had happened to be in London. We sat in Dad's living room. We went for dinner that night with Maranda and Sarah, to San Lorenzo in Knightsbridge. There was a time when Dad had gone there for lunch every day. He always had asparagus risotto. He and my mother had their wedding reception there when I was two months old.

The restaurant had become a parody of itself, like those Dolce Vita restaurants in Rome. The owner, Mara, was old and confined to her bed. Princess Diana, who loved the place, was dead. My dad, who loved the place, was dead. Maranda and I ate all our food, even though it was not good. Chryssoulla hardly ate. Sarah didn't eat at all. I wondered if she had found a new cocaine dealer, or maybe she still had some left from the last time she'd seen Dad. We drank a lot of wine and went back to Dad's flat afterwards, playing his rave compilation tapes, dancing in the living room. Sarah put a lace doily on her head and pranced around, no rhythm in her long arms.

'Dad would have loved this!' I shouted, sure that he was sitting on the sofa, watching, laughing, holding his walking stick, poised to stand up and join in.

Anthony called again. He wanted to come round and see the flat. He said he needed to work out what needed to be done to get the place ready for new tenants. I had been living in a limbo state halfway between reality and dream, death and life, imagining that I would always have his sofa, his bed. I had organized the printing of the order of service and the readings, I had taken his new black suit and a white shirt, still in its plastic dry-cleaning sleeve, to the undertakers so they could dress him. I crossed things off my list and added new ones: canapés, gravestone. But I had not organized clearing the flat.

At night I would come home and sit in the dark next to my baby whom I had not seen all day.

My mother said maybe you should stop drinking so much.

I sat in his bed and wrote him a letter. I cried as I wrote it. 'I love you so much, Dad. You went too soon, Dad.'

The wall separating life and death suddenly seemed very thin; there was a door in that wall, a handle that you could turn, open the door and walk through.

I finished writing the letter and I folded it many times to make it magic.

I found his hairdressing scissors in the wooden box in the living room, along with a grey plastic comb, a cut-throat razor, loose blades. He would need his scissors.

Sarah was waiting for me in the cab.

'Hello, darling,' she said. She had a tennis racket with her, for some reason.

'Are you ready?'

'Yes.'

The funeral parlour was on the Fulham Road. I now understood the geography of these things, hospital, funeral parlour, church, cemetery: all within ten minutes' walk of each other. Hidden pathways that only light up for the bereaved. The funeral parlour had glass windows so the immediate activities were visible to the people walking past, people who were not thinking about what wood to use for a coffin and whether to have shiny brass handles. At the next desk along was a woman who cried even as her credit card went through the machine. After she went they said to me, 'She's lost her baby. That's always the worst.'

This time the funeral men led me and Sarah through a door into a back room. More doors led to more rooms. These were the hidden spaces.

'He's in there,' they said, and one of them turned the handle and opened the door, so all I had to do was walk through.

Dad was in a coffin on a plinth, pushed up against the wall. He looked dapper, his grey hair brushed and fluffed.

I went to him; I looked at him; I laid my hand on his chest, solid and inanimate. I looked at his face, the familiarity of it, the little hamster pouches of fat, the flatness of his top lip, the grey of his eyelashes.

I retched with sobs.

'I love you so much,' I said.

I tucked the letter and the scissors into the front pocket of his suit. The funeral directors had Candy's ashes, and there was space for them at the foot of his coffin.

He had a small, quiet smile and his brow was smooth. I had not seen him look so untroubled for years. I knew that the funeral directors could do all sorts of things with the faces of the dead, but could they really make him look so content? He was not scared of death. And since Candy had died he had never been sure where he wanted to be more, there or here. He had given me twenty years and now he had gone to her.

I opened the door for Sarah.

She stood next to me and held my hand. Her fingers were bony and strong; she ground my knuckles together as though they were marbles.

'He looks happy,' she said.

'He does,' I said.

Sarah paid for Dad's last party. It was held at the Orangery in Holland Park, after his funeral in St Mary's and his interment in Brompton Cemetery. There were canapés, champagne, beautiful flowers, a soundtrack of Rolling Stones and early nineties acid house music. Everyone got drunk; we even had gatecrashers, people who turned up because they'd heard there was a good party happening, free booze and food, no problems getting in. Dad would have done the same. Once the last bottle had been drunk, the final stragglers, the 'die-hards' as Dad would have called them, went to Pucci's where we drank more and smoked and when someone offered me a line of cocaine I did not decline, even though I had a one-year-old baby at home. It seemed like the right thing to do, an act of homage. The night before dad died, they told me, he had taken cocaine, MDMA and smoked a couple of spliffs. He was having a party with his friends, playing two stereos at once, different music, had the telly on with the football as well.

I took the cocaine and felt the fireworks in my body and at the end of the night I went back to his flat and slept in his bed. My friend Lorna insisted on staying with me. She didn't think I should be on my own. I am not scared of my own ghosts, I thought, but I didn't say it and I was glad of the company.

I found the number of a man with a van who did flat clearances.

We talked through what I needed.

'I'll bring the truck,' he said.

He was Australian too. He was called Mark. He wore a blue Aertex shirt, cargo trousers and builder's boots. I made him a cup of tea, which he sipped quickly as he looked around the flat and worked out the scale of the job. I had taken home what I wanted, including the new television and Dad's diaries. I had given Sarah his crystals for her children, who'd loved him too; I had given Pucci's son Rufus his fantasy space station paintings. My mother had taken some of his nicer clothes to the charity shop. But there were still so many things to get rid of. Broken pans, stolen candles, porn videos, cushions and throws, house plants, six cans of steak and kidney pie, out-of-date medicines, bowls and bowls of photographs of me, him, Candy, the young girls he had supplied with drugs, alcohol, cigarettes.

We worked room by room, taking boxes and furniture down in the lift and throwing them into the cage on the back of the van. There were so many lovely things, beautiful mirrors, ornaments, his dressing table with the grey marble top which he had filled with mementos of lost loves. Lovely things that no one wanted and I could not take, lovely things that were him, his life, his joy. It broke my heart again and again to see them tumbling into the truck, becoming rubbish.

Anthony arrived while we were still clearing out.

Anthony was loose-limbed, fake-tanned, with thinning dyed black hair.

'This place is a fucking tip,' he said.

'We are just finishing up,' I said.

Mark, the man with the van, watched Anthony.

'Look at what's he done to the kitchen surfaces,' Anthony said, stroking the cracked Formica with his manicured hand. 'And there are cigarette burns in the carpet.'

'Dad was here for ten years,' I said.

Repairs were never done. Anthony was always aggressive with Dad. It was one of the few things that used to get him down.

'This whole place is going to need ripping out,' he muttered.

We walked up the carpeted stairs, Anthony first, me next, Mark following. There were long rectangular shapes on the purple-painted walls where my matriculation and graduation photographs had once hung. Dad had been so proud of me for going to Cambridge. He told everyone I got a first, even though I only got a 2:1; told everyone I was the editor of *ES*, even though I was only the deputy.

I watched as Anthony examined the bathroom door, the cracks in the wood where Sarah had bashed at it with the bronze elephant, the bronze elephant that was now on a bookshelf at home. My clean home where my husband and my baby lived, a place that had become so distant in my mind, like a faraway planet.

'Dad was locked in the loo when we found him.'

'This bathroom,' said Anthony.

The carpet around the base of the loo was crisp and yellowing from Dad's misdirected piss.

My soul hurt.

We went into the bedroom. Dad's bed was next to the window, which was half grown over with ivy. I knew what it was like, to lie in that bed and look out of that window. This was one of the nicest views in the flat, and for a time it had been mine.

I'd lived with Dad for a couple of years before moving in with Mike, and this had been my bedroom. In the evenings, when Mike would come round after a late night at work, when I would already be in bed, reading, Dad would let him in and invite him to hang out downstairs.

'Come and sit with us, have a drink,' he would say, and Mike would look through into the living room where three pretty Chelsea girls in their early twenties were sitting on the sofas, smoking, drinking cheap wine, snorting cocaine.

'No, thanks, I am going up to see Gavanndra.'

'Oh man, she's got you pussy-whipped!'

At our wedding in a converted youth hostel in Devon my father gave a speech. 'Hello, my name is Gavin and I am an addict. Oh no, wrong meeting!'

Laughter.

'We are here because of Gavanndra and Mike. They have something so special, something that I never had. Apologies, Jan!'

Laughter, even from my mother.

Dad liked to lie here and watch the birds through the greenery.

The bed was stripped; now it was just a stained mattress. The old duvets and pillows, the towels and sheets had been thrown away. The truck was nearly full.

'This bed isn't ours. This bed will have to go.'

'What?'

'This bed, and the one in the other room, you have to get rid of them.'

'I'm sure they were here when Dad took the place. I'm sure they're not his. This place was semi-furnished, wasn't it, when he took the place?'

'I'm telling you that these beds have to fucking go. You need to sort this out. We've given you loads of time. What have you been doing?'

'I . . . My . . .'

'This place is a fucking disgrace. Your father was a

slob. Disgusting. Don't imagine for a moment that you will be getting any deposit back.'

'My . . .'

My father is dead.

I looked out of the window, saw the truck outside, the rubbish cage filled to the brim, all his lovely things.

Mark was standing in the doorway.

Where was Dad? I hoped he wasn't watching this bit. I hoped he had gone by now, found Candy and the others. Andy; all his friends.

Mark stepped into the room. He walked with grace and confidence. 'Are you all right?' he said, looking at me.

I shook my head. That was all I could do. That was the honest truth.

'This has got nothing to do with you,' Anthony said to him.

Mark didn't stop walking until he faced Anthony, nose to nose. 'This girl's father has just died. You are a fucking bully. You know who is disgusting? You are, mate.'

Anthony's mouth quivered like he wanted to speak but didn't know what to say.

Mark took a small step closer so Anthony had to bend backwards. 'You're not going to pay her back her father's deposit. So she doesn't have to do shit. Why don't you just leave?'

Mark was right. Anthony had no power over me. I didn't have to do anything else here. I could leave. This empty place wasn't Dad's flat. It wasn't gone. It wasn't rubbish in a cage or stained mattresses. Dad's flat was in my head, I realized. In my head Dad could still sit on his sofa, drink wine, have a cigarette, play his music on his stereo, eat crème caramels in his kitchen, spray his house plants with water.

I heard Anthony stumble as he went down the stairs. He slammed the door behind him.

'Thank you,' I said to Mark.

'You're all right,' he replied.

33

2016, London

We are having a Christmas drinks party. It is mostly local friends, many of them parents from Hebe and Minna's school, people we chat to at drop-off and collection. It's a nice, gentle party. Prosecco and posh crisps. Mike is playing something jazzy on the record player; everyone has dressed up a bit, jewellery and lipstick.

I am in the living room, talking to a couple of people, including one of the more serious and high-flying mothers. She keeps looking above my head at the wall. I twist around to see what has caught her attention.

'What *is* that?' she asks.

Two of my dad's most treasured possessions were prints by Willy Feilding, a seventies artist whose central themes were dragons and sex. These prints were an important part of my childhood. I would stare at them for hours, fascinated by their intricate weirdness and explicit ribaldry. The prints are companion pieces; in the first a dragon with a massive erection looms over a maiden wearing nothing but a silky ribbon tied about her waist. This sacrifice/gift/lover is held aloft on a large pillow by a gaggle of naked and hirsute dwarf-like characters. She looks dreamily ecstatic; he (the dragon) ravenously lusty. In the second picture the dragon enters the maiden, who arches her back and tips her chin, an expression of faraway pleasure on her face, while he opens his dragon jaws and sticks out his pointy dragon tongue with crazed delight. The force of the inter-species lovemaking shakes the structure made by the dwarfs, who scatter and tumble, fire spurting from their penises.

It is this second 'copulation' image that hangs on the wall in my living room. I brought it home after Dad died.

'Ah, that belonged to my dad. It's a print, quite rare now. The artist has a sort of cult following – apparently Keith Richards collects a lot of his work.'

'Gosh,' she says, still staring at the picture. It takes a while to fully grasp what is going on.

'I got Mike to hang it up high so the girls can't see it properly. Normally no one notices it.'

I took so many things from Dad's flat after he died, trying to re-create the spirit of it in my own home (just like after Mum sold the flat in Battersea when I was twenty-one, and I had to re-create my childhood bedroom in various rental rooms across London). Dad loved knick-knacks, bits and bobs; he filled his flat with them to make it cosy, like a hobbit-hole. I do the same thing. But I think I do this to secure a sense of who I really am, my past charted in artefacts. After all, things are more trustworthy than memories, object not subject, archaeology not history. This painting, this little bronze elephant, this wooden carved box.

I took so many things from Dad's flat, including his

diaries and brown leather Filofax. He didn't really use it as a diary, more a place to collect mementos, mostly from the time when I was a teenager and his world suddenly became flooded with young girls. In it there are sexy drawings and secret messages, a collection of love letters tucked between the pages. The letters talk of 'heavenly union' and 'love of the most magical kind'. They talk about secrets, sex and longing. They also talk about homework that must be completed and parents who must be deceived.

My father said it all started one night when one of my friends was staying with us, even before Candy died. She and I were up watching television. It was late and we were just in our nighties. She was wearing a loose T-shirt that fell off her shoulders and a pair of white pants. She was golden and beautiful, loose and languid. Dad would later tell me that night was 'when the dragon woke up'. As a heroin addict he'd had no sex drive, he told me; when he was newly sober he'd had no sex drive, he told me; Mum had put on weight so he didn't fancy her any more, he told me (he always told me too much). But just looking at my friend's youthful body and the thoughtless, trusting touch of a naked thigh against his leg, that was enough to rouse his dormant sex beast.

Nothing happened, not at first. He looked; he admired; he made friends with my friends. He talked to them as no other adult talked to them. He was funny, generous, full of street wisdom. I loved him and felt special for having a dad like him. All my friends envied me my father.

But after my sister died the renewal of his sexual urges coalesced with another kind of longing, a longing for lost little girls. The two things seemed to become confused in his mind. At the end of Dad's Filofax there is an in-built wallet; inside is a collection of onion-skin-thin receipts from the hotel in Tunisia, including one for a pancake, signed by Candy Hodge in joined-up handwriting. He kept this in his diary, along with those love letters from teenaged girls. All his lost little girls.

Candy's death might be an explanation for some of my father's behaviour but, unlike my mother, I don't think it is an excuse. He gave drugs to those girls. Girls who were my friends. Girls who went to my school. Girls whom I brought down to his hairdressing salon. Their parents thought their children were safe because of me. But I couldn't keep anyone safe.

I thought that I might want to write about the strange sexual politics of the late eighties and early nineties, how sexual relationships between young girls and older men seemed normalized, fetishized even, all over the newspapers, Bill Wyman and Mandy Smith. I could write about how we competed for the attentions of older men, how older men thought our bodies were available to them, perhaps because we seemed to be offering them, even though what we were really doing was play-acting, because we were children. But that just feels like me finding more ways to excuse my father's behaviour and I don't want to do that any more.

The imagery still astonishes me, that he thought of his sex drive like a mythical creature that lived within him and could not be controlled once it had been unleashed: wild and glorious, winged and ferocious.

My father never said sorry. The drug addiction was a disease; the sex drive was a dragon. It's not my fault, he told me, again and again. It's not my fault, my darling, it's the dragon.

And yet I still have that Willy Feilding print hanging on my wall. Why don't I take it down and sell it? Why do I keep it in my home, endangering the shiny happy world that my husband and I have created for our children? Cut out the rotten nastiness and leave only the healthy goodness. Is that the answer? Is that how it works?

I don't think so. Not for me at least.

I have the Willy Feilding print because it is as much a part of me as my Latin texts (which I also still have). Order and chaos, life and death, past and future. These opposites must be accommodated and held in a state of balanced oscillation. I love my dad and I am furious with him. One of the hardest things for me is accepting who he really was. I cannot just pretend that he was fun and funny, because he was also dangerous and manipulative and hurt people in ways that are unforgivable. This is painful and lonely knowledge. I wish I had someone who understands how it feels to be a daughter of a man like him.

But I do.

My father had two Willy Feilding prints. They are companion pieces. I have one. The other is in Los Angeles.

34

2016, London and Los Angeles

I have eaten smoked salmon, tender steak and dauphin-oise potatoes. I have drunk champagne and too much expensive red wine. I am wearing a dress that sheds gold glitter all over the grey-carpeted floor. It is a fashion dinner and I am having fun with people I barely know in a private room in a posh new Scandinavian restaurant in St James's.

Someone strikes their glass with a silver teaspoon.

'I'd just like to say thank you all so much for coming, it means so much to me that we can share this magical day. What I would like for us to do now is to take a moment to reflect on our blessings, and perhaps we could go around the table and everyone could raise a toast to someone or something that is really meaningful to them.'

The woman speaking is a towering blonde, a former model turned fashion designer, an Americanized European.

For God's sake, I think, refilling my glass so that there will be enough wine for me to toast every sodding blessing around the table. They toast and I drink. They toast and I drink. Again and again.

Now it is my turn and they are all looking at me and I have no idea what to say.

'This is deeply embarrassing for me because I am British.' I pause, allowing everyone to laugh at my dry British wit. 'But I would like to raise a toast,' I say. 'To sisters.'

They all cheer and raise their glasses high above their heads before drinking enthusiastically. Maranda, who is sitting next to me, clinks her glass against mine a second time, a private salutation, one meant only for us.

'To sisters,' she says.

After our father's death Maranda and I saw each other a couple of times. She would come to London for a premiere or work-related event. We would hang out for a few hours, get drunk, make promises to see each other more, to be in contact more, promises that we did not keep.

Maranda had become so folded up in the mayhem of Candy's death, my father's behaviour, all the chaos, sadness and hardship, that I forgot she was my sister too.

And now here we are again, meeting in the dislocated way that we always do, a random fancy event, where I get drunk and do something embarrassing (like the film party where I tried to kiss the actor John Hamm at 2 a.m.), this time a dinner to celebrate the launch of a range of weird floaty black clothing designed by one of Maranda's friends.

'I'm writing a book, actually, it's a sort of autobiographical thing,' I say between mouthfuls of chocolate mousse.

'That's amazing!' replies Maranda.

'I'm planning a writing trip for spring next year. I need to get away so I can concentrate. It's so hard, with work and the kids and everything.'

'Come and stay with me in Los Angeles,' says Maranda immediately.

'That would be great – I would love that,' I reply, not knowing if I mean the words I am saying, but knowing that they are the right ones to say.

Over the next couple of months Maranda emails me.

'When are you coming to LA? Have you booked your flights?'

'I just need to sort a few things out!'

What I don't say is that I have also been in touch with the spa editor of the magazine and that we are discussing a trip to Nepal, eight days of trekking in the mountains, with my very own guide and yoga instructor, staying with local families, the final few days in a luxury lodge where, apparently, the air is so clear that the stars and dense galaxies that light the night sky look as though they are within touching distance. It's a once-in-a-lifetime trip; I just have to pay for the flights and write a short piece for the magazine. I can only do one major trip away from my family a year, and this year it will be Nepal. I can do LA any time, I reason. But to walk in the Himalayas with my own guide and yoga teacher, to touch the stars . . .

I have selected my flights and am still answering Maranda's emails with a jaunty 'just sorting everything out!'

In the middle of January, two weeks before I am due to go to Nepal, the boutique travel company organizing the trip emails me with final confirmations. The email lists all the vaccinations that are required: yellow fever, dengue fever, malaria tablets, various other terrifying-sounding diseases. The breezy tone assumes that as a seasoned adventure traveller I will have had most of these jabs already.

I am not an adventurous traveller. I find holidays scary. Terrible things happen to me on holiday. I have never been vaccinated against a tropical disease.

I realize that I am more scared of spending a week with my sister than I am of going to Nepal. I realize this is both mad and a mistake. The trip to Nepal isn't the trip of a lifetime. The trip to Los Angeles might be.

I cancel the Himalayas trip, pissing everyone off, and book last-minute tickets to Los Angeles. I feel huge relief when I do this, like a balloon that has been let go and is gently floating into uncharted places.

It's the longest flight I have ever taken. I am wild with nerves. Connecting with a living lost sister suddenly seems so much harder than all the things I have done in search of a dead one.

Maranda and her daughter Biba are waiting for me in the arrivals hall of LAX looking excited. And the first thing I notice, the first surprise, is Biba. I haven't seen her since she was a baby and now that she is grown she looks so much like Hebe. They are the same age and they look more like sisters than me and Maranda. It amazes me that the universe could play such a clever trick, so that I will love her immediately.

The other surprise, which I keep secret at first, because it feels like something illicit, is how much Maranda reminds me of Dad. I notice it straightaway, as we drive from the airport to Palm Springs (where Maranda has a styling job the next day). The way she drives, her legs slightly apart, energetic and muscular, going too fast, overtaking while talking, the music too loud. The way she sits in the driver's seat is the way he sat in a driver's seat. It does not end there. Maranda's house in Silverlake has a basement that she has converted into a hairdressing salon, and walking into it feels like walking into my father's basement salon in Knightsbridge. She has his pictures, his brushes, all the things she took when she came to London after he died. It is like stepping into the shimmering space between past and present. And when we go walking in the hills around Los Angeles, me always following in her wake, I realize that her body is my father's body, she has his shoulders, his neck, his neat bottom, his calf muscles, big and strong like bunched fists. Walking around the Silverlake Wholefoods with Maranda and Biba I have this feeling of reconnection with my father again, watching her fill a paper bag with big chocolate-covered nuts, taking two more from the dispenser and popping one into Biba's mouth, one into her own. Listening to her stories, listening to the way she takes the truth and weaves it into something crazy and exciting, that's him too.

'I had over one hundred thousand dollars. I'd been working like hell to save for years, so I could open a salon, and he stole it all from me. This guy that I was in love with, and I don't think he even liked me. I couldn't get the money back from him, I couldn't go back to Stockholm like a failure, so I played backgammon for money with the guys on Miami Beach. I hustled. Here is the tattoo I got for that time.'

A pair of dice, two sixes, on the soft skin of her inner arm.

I listen to all her wild stories, open-mouthed, loving hearing them, not caring that there might be a gap between reality and exaggeration. That gap doesn't matter to the daughters of Gavin Hodge, that gap is where the magic is.

Maranda made enough money in Miami to come to LA, made contacts, worked hard, and now she is one of the most successful session hairdressers in the city. She bought her beautiful house, with its garden full of palm trees and succulents, a Balinese day bed and a hot tub. She has never depended on anyone else, never been given a penny. 'Work Bitch' by Britney Spears is one of her favourite songs, played at top volume in her massive Mercedes SUV as we drive to hot yoga.

On the Friday before I am due to return to London we spend an afternoon at the twenty-four-hour Wi Spa in Koreatown. Maranda, Biba and I plunge into pools that are, by turn, hot, unbearably hot, cold and unbearably cold. We are naked, all three of us, our skin pink and sleek, as we walk from pool to pool. We chat, submerged from the chin down, like hippos at a watering hole. We observe the nakedness of the other women, the various shaped breasts, the tattoos, the abundance or scarcity of pubic hair. We sweat in the steam room, the steam hissing out of unseen vents; and afterwards Maranda and I lie on marble slabs, naked, while middle-aged Korean women in black underwear scrub us with soap and mitts, under our breasts, in our armpits, between our toes, so that not a scrap of old skin remains. Biba stands by my marble slab and watches as the grey strings of dead skin peel off my pale British body to be swept on to the floor. There is a lot of dead skin, enough to fill a couple of big cups.

'What's that stuff?' asks Biba.

'It's all my old skin. I'll be a kilo lighter after this!' I say.

'But why do you have so much? My mom doesn't have so much.'

'In England we don't have Korean spas, so we don't get the chance to be this clean,' I reply.

Maranda believes in cleanliness. She tells me that the awfulness of living with us in Battersea, the dirt and grime, the casual degradation of our flat, brought out her OCD. She cleans her kitchen surfaces with anti-bacterial wipes many times a day.

In some ways Maranda is like my father and in some ways she is like me, grappling with the past. But mostly she is herself.

Afterwards we pat ourselves dry with many towels, put on the baggy shorts and yellow T-shirts that were provided on arrival and leave the women-only area for the communal hall. This is a large, high-ceilinged space with a heated floor and beige marble tiles where people loll on mats, read, chat, nap, watch their devices with headphones in. Maranda finds some mats and an empty corner and produces the face masks she has purchased for us: damp, slithery sheets of thick tissue which have been infused with moisturizer, serums and peptides to make skin more youthful looking. There are holes for the nose, mouth and eyes, and the masks have to be smoothed on to the face so the wearer looks like an Egyptian mummy or a burns victim or someone recovering from a serious cosmetic procedure. Maranda squeezes some extra serum from the packets into my palm.

'Here, put this on your neck,' she says.

I am not used to being looked after. I am not used to having an older sister. But I have decided to let Maranda take charge. I will play the role of a younger sister for the first time in my life. I rub the transparent gunge on to my neck.

We lounge on the cushioned mats, the heat rising through the marble floor, the beautifying masks slicked to our faces.

Biba sits a little way away from us, also wearing a face mask, even though she does not need it because she is not quite nine, watching cartoons on her iPad. I feel so carefree and happy. I don't think that I have felt this way for a long time, perhaps ever.

'Do you remember we had matching velvet jump-suits, with a little zip up the front, mine was yellow, yours was brown?' Maranda says.

'No, I don't remember,' I say.

'I was staying with you in the flat in Battersea for a bit, when we were really small. It was one night and the police were banging on the door. Dad gave us drugs to hold – he pushed the bags into our hands and then shoved us into the bathroom and shut the door. I remember being in that bathroom and looking down at you, at your blonde hair, you must have been about four, so I would have been about six, and I thought to myself, I cannot look after her, I cannot, because I am too small, and it makes me so sad.'

'I don't remember that at all,' I say, and I find that I am crying a little, my tears absorbed by the mask. I am crying for many reasons, but mostly because I have discovered that someone else shares my experiences, someone else wanted to look after me when I was too small to look after myself. And it feels like walking through a door into a place that belongs to me but I never knew I had, a beautiful open place where I feel free.

Maranda has another gift for me. A memory of Candy. I explain how I can't remember her.

'I remember her,' says Maranda. 'I remember that she used to drive us mad. If we were trying to watch something on television she would stand in front of it and try to get our attention. She would not stop, even if we shouted at her.'

There is a photograph of Maranda in Marbella that occasionally appears on social media, Maranda as a chubby baby, naked but for a sunhat with a strap that goes under her chin, held by our father, who is showing her off to his long-haired, beaded, bohemian friend Mim. The comments underneath include an anecdote about a day Gavin and Kerstin went walking in the scrubby hills above Marbella with their new baby. They had neglected to take food, drink and milk. Soon enough baby Maranda began to cry, distressed by the heat, the noise of the crickets, the dry haze that rose from the bare, sharp earth. The adventurous, ill-prepared couple came upon a shepherd and this shepherd allowed Maranda to drink fresh milk from one of his goats. I imagine Kerstin and Gavin holding her under the goat so she could suck at a pink teat, warm milk dribbling down her cheeks, a tiny goddess, a founder of civilizations.

I like this story very much. I am even slightly envious of it. I feel like a weakling compared to my sister. She has survived so much. 'For me, Dad was the sane one,' she says, and I cannot imagine what that must have been like.

Maranda hasn't heard from her mother for three years. Kerstin is still a drug addict, an alcoholic, the sort of person you see sitting on a bench with a bottle of vodka. The last time Maranda was in Stockholm she went to the flat where her mother lived, knocked on the door, called out. She could hear that someone was in the flat – her mother, she assumed – but no one answered the door.

'It is my birthday tomorrow and I know my mum won't even get in touch. But now you are here and I am so happy,' she says, and she starts to cry.

On Maranda's birthday we go to a terrifyingly sweaty SoulCycle class in Hollywood, we go to the shooting range in Burbank, we get matching tattoos, three birds for three sisters, and that night we get drunk at dinner with all her glamorous friends, who seem to include every famous Swedish person in Hollywood, including the actresses Malin Akerman and Britt Ekland.

*

Five months later, for the summer holidays, Maranda comes to England with Biba, who has never met her cousins before. We rent a house in Aldeburgh and eat chips on the beach in the rain. Hebe and Biba and Minna play and argue, run into a cold sea together, collect stones on the beach, the special ones with the hole in the middle.

'Those are called hag stones,' I explain. 'They are magic. If you look through the hole you might be able to see ghosts.'

Later in 2017 Maranda's mother, Kerstin, dies in deeply unpleasant circumstances involving drugs. Maranda cannot face returning to Stockholm to deal with this. Biba's father (from whom Maranda is amicably separated) asks his mother to help clear out the flat, which is, apparently, shockingly horrible.

In 2018 I go to LA for my birthday. Maranda takes me to Joshua Tree National Park, we drink home-made absinthe with her friends, she cuts my hair into a sharp bob and on the evening of my birthday she asks one of her Tinder dates to take us to the Magic Castle to watch card tricks, illusionists and mind-readers. That summer Maranda organizes a beautiful farewell ceremony for her mother in Sweden, commissioning a bouquet in the shape of angel wings. Maranda tells me that now her mother is dead she finally feels free to be herself. She says she always felt unloved, unwanted, too much.

There is a bag of letters that have been found in Kerstin's apartment, ones that our father wrote to Kerstin when he was stuck in Marbella with a broken leg and she had returned to Sweden. As the self-appointed family archivist I am the one to go through the letters (on another trip to LA). I am astonished by the neatness of Dad's handwriting and how desperately he loved Kerstin. I find the letter Dad wrote to her after he learnt that she was pregnant and that she was considering an abortion. 'Please! Please! Keep <u>our</u> baby!' he writes. 'Look,' I say, showing Maranda. 'You were wanted.' She frames the letter and hangs it in her bathroom.

In the summer of 2018 Maranda and Biba visit the UK again. We go glamping in Devon, Maranda sitting on the pebble beach in Sidmouth wearing her skimpy black bikini, LA tan, gold jewellery (including Dad's chain), perfect manicure, peroxide-blonde hair, multiple tattoos, buying the girls the biggest ice-creams she can find and laughing at the morris dancers who have congregated on the seafront. When we come back to London I take Maranda and Biba to see Dad and Candy's grave, where we leave one of the hag stones we collected in Suffolk the summer before.

Three sisters in the same place for the first time in so many years.

35

2018, London

My mother has been hospitalized three more times since she got sepsis, once when she fell and broke her ankle taking the girls to school, and twice for other less serious falls. She walks with a stick now and is unsteady on her feet. She is still beautiful, though, her undyed hair barely grey, her violet-coloured eyes still changeable. She likes wearing jewel-coloured clothes and swanky shawls. She gets a fair bit of romantic attention at church.

And she still babysits for the girls, always bringing them a bar of her favourite dark chocolate (which she insists is healthy). Sometimes she will mistakenly call my older daughter Gavanndra and my younger daughter Candy.

The girls love their nanny. She likes to go shopping with them, and lets them buy whatever impractical and sparkly outfits they desire. Minna wore the Supergirl swimming costume (complete with red netting skirt) my mother bought her constantly for about three years, even to swimming classes.

Sometimes my mother seems giddy and girlish to me. She does not have much sense with money, even though she is a trained accountant. She invested all her savings in an apartment in Spain just before a property crash. My father stayed in the apartment, by himself, six weeks before he died. He'd had a bad chest infection and thought that the dry, sunny climate would be good for his health. Mum says that after he came back he suggested they remarry. She doesn't know if he was joking. She thinks he probably just wanted to spend more time in her apartment in Spain. She had to sell it a couple of years after he died for a lot less than she bought it for.

My mother has God and she has us.

She also has the memory of Candy.

It has taken me three years of writing, reading, imagining, grieving and various other therapies to feel brave enough to talk to my mother about my sister. But finally I am ready. I don't feel scared any more. I only feel curious. Impatient even.

I walk to her flat on a crisp and chilly day, just like the one I spent with my daughters in the playground outside the Horniman Museum. My mother and I sit on comfortable chairs in her sitting room and I ask her to tell me about the daughter she lost.

'She was a very pretty baby, just like you. She was an adventurous little thing. When she was fifteen months old, she climbed up the big plant we had in the sitting room. I was in the kitchen making her lunch and I heard this almighty crash. When I found her she was underneath the heavy plant pot. Her leg was fractured and she had to have a plaster cast. She had only just started walking and had to go back to crawling. Every so often she would say to me, "Do you remember when I had to crawl around with my leg?" And I would say, "Yes, and do you remember climbing up the flipping tree!" '

I laugh and so does Mum. She does not seem sad to be talking about Candy; she seems to be enjoying herself. I ask what Candy looked like, how she dressed.

'She was a very flamboyant child. She always wore her big pink coat and her shoes undone. Sometimes, when I was taking her to school, I would walk a few paces behind her because she looked so extraordinary. As long as I could see her, I thought it was all right.'

I cannot remember walking to school with Candy, I only remember going by myself, taking the bus over the bridge, my keys in my school bag, always so independent and self-contained. I think what I learnt, very early on, was that I was the only person I could depend on. But Candy didn't feel that way.

'She was not as academic as you – it took her longer to learn to read – but she was very artistic, she loved dancing and swimming. She had very close friends.

'I wouldn't say that she was bossy, but she would never do anything she didn't want to do. Once, during a swimming lesson, the instructor told her to put her face in the water. She said no, and he said, "Come on, put your face in the water, it's all right."

' "No."

' "Really, it is OK, put your face in."

'So she just climbed out of the teaching pool and went to the big pool and started playing there. It was the same with her tutor; she really ruled the roost with him. Once, she had done some work and then called out, "Mummy, I would like a cup of tea." And I said, "No. When you have finished you can have a cup of tea, darling." So she tore up the work she had done. The tutor, who was only a young guy, was like "Ooh! What are we going to do with her?"'

I had a different tutor, an old man with dangling BFG ears who smelt of instant coffee and would show me how to solve maths problems with a sharpened pencil. I took our lessons very seriously. I cannot imagine being the sort of person who would tear up a piece of work on a whim. We must have been so different.

'She was more attached to her cuddly toys than you. She was very careful with all her dolls. She would say, "There is no point in having a baby if you don't look after it properly." She was very precious about her things. I think the worst occasion for her was when the police came to search the flat. They went through all her stuff, and took her dollies' hats off their heads to look for drugs. She was very particular about how her dolls were arranged, so that was just a complete nightmare for her, poor little sausage.

'At night I would sometimes have to sit beside her for hours before she would go to sleep, and then when she was seven or eight years old she started to share a bed with us. She didn't want independence. She wanted to stay close to us.'

Mum starts to look sad. She reaches for a tissue and blows her nose.

'I think she had some kind of spiritual knowledge that she didn't have very long with us. From a very early age she would say, "I am never going to live anywhere but with you and Daddy. I am not going to grow up," and I would say, "Can you not say that, darling, I don't like it."'

'Oh, Mum,' I say.

But as heartbreaking as this conversation is, it is also beautiful. Just as I gave my daughters memories of Candy, my mother is giving me memories of her, placing them gently in my mind, bringing her to life.

I turn off the Dictaphone and we look through the red leather-bound photograph album that my parents compiled after Candy died, filled with pictures of her looking mad, fun, wild, happy, sad. Her school reports are also stuck in the album and I read these aloud.

1986
Candy is one of the youngest children in her age group. She has been very immature but recently her attitude and concentration on her work has suddenly improved. Her written content is good but her thoughts run away with her and she leaves out words.

1987
Candida gets on well with her peer group and has some special long-standing friendships. She enjoys school and is always willing and eager to take part in all the activities offered.

1988
Candy is usually a very helpful girl. She can be a little aggressive towards other children if they cross her but generally she is kind.

I feel if she listened and concentrated without being distracted she would make better progress. She needs lots of help and encouragement with her reading and lots of positive confidence-building.

1989

Candy speaks very well and should try not to use the babyish voice she uses sometimes. She has recently shown a great interest in writing stories so perhaps this will help her reading, which she finds rather a chore . . . Candida is outgoing and loving. She works enthusiastically if not always with care. She loves to paint and her work has improved tremendously over the year. She still needs to give a lot more attention to her reading. She has a tremendous sense of fun and is well liked by her peers. I have enjoyed her larger-than-life personality.

And then I suggest that we open Candy's box.

After my father left home to live in Putney my parents could not agree who should have Candy's box, so it came to me. I had it in my bedroom, by my bed. I kept my little black-and-white portable television on it, my glasses, ashtray, cigarettes, usually a cup of tea. I didn't like the box. Sometimes when I was pissed or high I imagined it was full of toys that were decaying, melting Barbie dolls and mouldering pink fluff. The exterior might look all right, especially when I polished it, but inside was hell, just like me.

When my mother sold our flat, the autumn after I graduated from Cambridge, and I had to move out of home, my parents agreed that my father would have Candy's box and ashes and my mother would have the photograph album. Over a decade later my father died. Candy's ashes were buried with him and her box was returned to my mother.

It has never been opened.

'If you like,' says Mum. 'If we can open it. You lost the key, remember.'

'I didn't lose the key!'

'Well, that was how it came to me, without the key.'

'It would have been Dad who lost the key.'

The key doesn't matter – it was only ever ornamental. I find a long match and poke it into the fancy bronze lock. It springs apart.

The box was packed messily by my parents, in grief, during a time that was harrowing and unreal. I kneel by the box and begin to pull things out, item by item, my mother watching. I lay the items on her bed, fluffy chick puppets, a wicker box containing pencils, a mirror, a lipstick without its lid, wet-look gel and a large safety pin, her straw hat, her ruler with her name written on the back in pencil, a recorder, a tape of the *Dirty Dancing* soundtrack, her purse containing twenty-two pence in coins and a shilling, a fluffy panda, a hand-sewn felt dog with a plastic bead necklace, a yellow neon hairband, a foam red nose, a glass elephant ornament, a screen print of a butterfly, goggles, the rubber perishing, two pairs of sunglasses, brown fluffy bear-foot slippers with soft claws, a pink bikini, a red swimming costume, a swathe of pink chiffon that I recognize from a photograph of her in a school show, a bar of fancy soap in its plastic case, various other fluffy animals, a smudged red lipstick kiss on a white napkin, a tape measure, a small plastic Donald Duck, two identical plastic dolls with pink hair and sunglasses, a flower press, the album of tributes from her funeral, the clothes she wore the day before she died, a pink skirt and white broderie anglaise sleeveless top. The hood from her pink coat.

My mother picks up her bikini.

'It's so small,' she says. 'The dear girl,' she says.

And she sits on the bed and sobs and I hug her and cry too.

Candy's things are so much more powerful than any words. They radiate her individuality. Here is a person; here is a short life, mapped in possessions.

I arrange her things on the bed so that we can look at them all, pick them up, remember them, remember her, then I pack them away neatly, leaving the box unlocked. I take one of the plastic dolls with the pink hair and sunglasses, and my mother takes the other. This doll seems to contain so much of Candy's personality: fun, flamboyant, devil-may-care. I put her in my handbag and take her to the theatre that night to see Angela Carter's *Wise Children*, Candy balanced on the red velvet armrest next to me. I think she enjoys it, after being shut in the darkness for so long.

One of my favourite myths isn't Greek or Roman, it is Egyptian, the story of the goddess Isis and her brother

Osiris. As well as being brother and sister, Isis and Osiris were husband and wife. They also had a brother called Seth, who envied Osiris and made many attempts to kill him. Seth would do terrible things, like locking his brother in a jewelled coffin and tossing him into the sea. But Isis always managed to save Osiris. Finally Seth decided to thwart Isis by chopping Osiris's body into fourteen pieces and spreading the chunks throughout Egypt, up and down the Nile, to make sure he could never be put back together. But Isis was determined to find every last bit of her brother and she travelled the kingdom, hunting for his remains. Eventually she found them all and laid the pieces of Osiris on the ground. She used spices and magic to bind him together, to make the bones fuse and the muscles tighten. She wrapped him in bandages, spoke elaborate spells and words of love, and his stilled heart began to beat and the blood to flow in his veins, so his eyes could flutter open and his brain recognize that he was alive and that above him was the face of Isis, looking anxious and beautiful.

'We haven't got long,' she whispered, and he saw that she was naked, her skin glowing bronze, and he became excited. She lowered herself on to him and they made love for the last time, his god sperm meeting her goddess egg. Because no magic, no power was strong enough to undo what Seth had done. Once Osiris had laid his hands on his wife's lovely stomach and felt the life that was growing within it, his head dropped back and he breathed his last earth-bound breath. Osiris was now consigned to the underworld, but his presence was still on the earth, in the form of the new god that he and Isis had made, Horus, their son, who would rule above while his father ruled below.

It's an extraordinary tale. And the most extraordinary thing about it is that the Egyptians were afraid to tell it. The story of Isis and Osiris was one of the foundation myths of their society, a violent tale of death, love and rebirth, but the Egyptians thought it so powerful and terrifying that they did not like to write it down or to speak it. They thought that the magic act of remembering the story might enable it to happen again. They would not talk about it.

I was once scared of my story. I didn't want to speak the words, not because I literally believed that speaking would make everything happen again, not in the real world, but in my head. And that was bad enough.

But in order to find Candy, in order to start living and stop surviving, in order to feel love, I had to feel grief, I had to start remembering and telling.

I might not have found a cache of hidden memories during that process, a pop-up book of a person that was hidden in the depths of my subconscious, all complete and waiting for me to open it, but I have found other things. I have brought Candy to life in a different way. I have gathered all the pieces of her and put them together so that now I know her once more. I have my sister. She lives inside of me, in my bones and my blood, just as she is in my children. And the crazy thing is that she was here all along, waiting, impatient, I just had to look at the world in a different way to find her. Just as my other sister, Maranda, was always here, waiting, impatient. All I had to do was unlock myself, allow myself to feel again, to leave that hotel room in Tunisia, walk down the long strange corridor, out of the lonely darkness and into the sunshine.

Epilogue

2019, London

It is spring. Our garden is filled with abundant life, blossom and primroses, unfurling fresh foliage, buzzing pollinators and floating pollen. My children are bouncing on the tree-shaded trampoline in our back garden, shouting and laughing. Minna lies on the trampoline so that she will be bounced while Hebe jumps. I watch them from the kitchen window. It looks like a kind of paradise out there.

I have often wondered who I might have been were it not for my childhood. Who was that little girl before she started understanding that her world was not safe, before she began making the psychological adjustments that understanding required (I have read books that suggest these adjustments begin in the womb). There have been times when I have grieved for that innocent girl, the one who trusted the world, the version of me that has been lost.

One of the emotions that I associate most strongly with my father is disappointment. He never stopped disappointing me. I think this is a feeling that most children of addicts will understand. We forgive, we hope, we are disappointed, again and again, until disappointment becomes an emotion that is woven into our psyche.

My father continues to disappointment me. The more I think about the things he did, the long impact of his actions, not just on my life, but on those of the other people, the more I condemn him. He damaged people and that damage lives on even though he is gone. I cannot change that, even though I wish so much that I could. And it was only once he was gone that I was able to start thinking about his behaviour properly. Finally grieving for my sister also required me to face up to hard truths about my father. I am trying not to let those truths crush me. I hope I will succeed.

Disappointment is an interesting emotion – flip it on its head and you find something different. Hope. We are only ever disappointed because we were hopeful that something good was going to happen, because we believed that things would be better next time, even though life keeps showing us that that is unlikely, again and again. This may be blind, insane, irrational, but it is also essential for survival.

I am an optimist, always have been. That is what I share with the girl I was before; that is the part of me which could not be changed by experience. The certainty that somehow, some way, things would turn out all right.

My optimism could not be unlearnt. Whoever I was before (whenever that was), one thing is certain: I was the kind of child, the kind of individual, who would be able to deal with the life that she was given. That is who I was. That is who I am. She is not lost. She is me.

Author's Note

This is a book about memory and trauma. Memory informs who we are, how we think and how we act. It is essentially an evolutionary process: we remember so we know how to behave next time; we forget so that we are not stuck in the past, so we can move on. In that sense memory is about the future.

And then we turn our memories into 'stories'. We all do this, as individuals and as families. The stories we tell about ourselves, again and again, are the threads that knit us together. The processes that move incident to memory to story are alchemical and transformative, tracking forwards and backwards. Each time we tell a story about a moment in our lives, each time we write it down, or talk it through with a therapist, our memory of that moment is subtly altered.

Memory is not static or fixed: it moves through our bodies like liquid; it changes as we change; often it is beyond our control. The way I remember my sister's death now, over thirty years after the event, is different to the way I remembered it days after it happened. Different people who were in the same place on the same day watching the same thing happen remember it differently. Who we are affects how we see.

One of the most interesting consequences of writing this book was the conversation I had with my mother after she read it. It was hard to write this book, and it was hard for my mother to read it. She did it slowly, taking it in small chunks, and I would call every few days to make sure she was OK. She made notes on the manuscript and many of the comments that she made have been integrated into the book – what I wore on the day of my sister's funeral, for instance, or the fact it was she, and not my father, who paid for the extravagant dinner in Vale do Lobo. But there were other discrepancies in our recollections which I have left in the text because I find it interesting that our memories diverge: I remember the policeman pulling Candy's teddy bear apart during the raid; my mother said he removed her dolls' hats. In another divergence, my mother says that on the holiday in Portugal she found the letter from Julia, along with a necklace belonging to her. She says she tore up the letter, broke the necklace, left these on my father's bed (according to her they did not share a bedroom during this trip), and waited until the next day to confront him. But I have a powerful memory of finding her sitting there, reading the letter and asking me to fetch him. The 'truth', I imagine, is somewhere between our two recollections.

A couple of incidents have been conflated (mostly the drunken, druggie evenings, which all tend to merge into one in my head). I have left out some people who were present at dinners and on holidays, because I wanted to focus on my family. Some names and identifying details have been changed to preserve anonymity. The rest is as I remember it.

Acknowledgements

Thank you to my agent Lizzy Kremer for her huge empathy and intelligence, and for giving me the confidence to do it; thank you to my editor Fenella Bates, who is both incredibly clever and incredibly kind. Thank you to Louise Moore for believing in this book; to Laura Nicol, Jennifer Breslin, Rachel Myers and the rest of the team at Michael Joseph, who have been brilliant throughout

Thank you to all the friends who have read this book at various points in its creation, and who have given me the advice and encouragement I needed: Tanya Brett, Julia Churchill, Hermione Eyre, Tonia George, Zoe King, Imogen Martineau, Harriet Moore, Victoria Moore, Kate Pakenham, Clementine Pillai, Annabel Rivkin, Naomi Rokotnitz, Sasha Slater, Therese Steele, Matthew Sweet, Stuart Williams, Andrew Wilson and Angharad Wood. Thank you to Clare Bennett for spotting my mistake about *The Iliad*, and to Kate Reardon for pointing out that San Lorenzo's did not take credit cards. Thank you to Emilie McMeekan who read EVERY SINGLE version of the book and somehow managed to maintain her enthusiasm when even I had lost mine. Thank you to Ross Barr, Laura Jones and Fiona McKinney for maintaining my sanity. Thank you to John Vial and Debbie Bhowmik for looking after the daughter of a hairdresser who lost her dad.

Thank you to Maranda for being my fabulous and indomitable sister – what adventures we will have! Thank you to my mother for her boundless love and care, and for being so open-hearted and brave. Thank you to Hebe, Minna and Mike, for making me feel safe enough, and loved enough, to write this story.